Mangia Bene!

NEW AMERICAN FAMILY COOKBOOKS

Capital's cooking series that focuses on treasured Old Country family recipes and how they are changed by new blended American families in our increasingly diverse culture.

Other titles include:

¡Sabroso! A Spanish American Family Cookbook
by Noemi Cristina Taylor

NEW AMERICAN FAMILY COOKBOOKS

Mangia Bene!

The Italian American Family Cookbook

KATE DEVIVO

CAPITAL BOOKS, INC.
STERLING, VIRGINIA

Capital Books, Inc.
P.O. Box 605
Herndon, Virginia 20172-0605

Design and composition by Melissa Ehn
at Wilsted & Taylor Publishing Services

LIBRARY OF CONGRESS CATALOGING-IN-PUBLICATION DATA

DeVivo, Kate.
  Mangia Bene!: the Italian American family cookbook / Kate DeVivo.
    p. cm.
  ISBN 1-892123-85-1
  1. Cookery, Italian.   I. Title.
  TX723.D435 2003
  641.5945—dc21   2002017424

Printed in the United States of America on acid-free paper that meets the American National Standards Institute Z39-48 Standard.

First Edition

10 9 8 7 6 5 4 3 2 1

For Grandma,
who passed on more than recipes
through her cooking lessons.

CONTENTS

PREFACE

I began this book about five years ago while I was working at a cookbook publishing company. I had been living in Chicago for a year, was cooking for myself, and found that the cookbooks I had were limited in scope and variety. Although my college years hardly found me craving much beyond a meal that included a bagel or pretzels and two Diet Cokes, now that I was out in the working world (and editing recipes all day), I began longing for my mom's meals, my Grandma's goodies, and all the fantastic foods I had grown up with.

I decided to put together a cookbook of family recipes for myself, and began by collecting the Italian classics from my dad's side of the family—Grandma's pizza, spaghetti and meatballs, stuffed artichokes, pizzelles. I wrote to many family members and asked them to send me some of their favorite recipes, especially any they had from Grandma. They sent a bunch of recipes, including many different variations of Grandma's, but I wanted authenticity, so I went straight to the source. I spent a week with Aunt Anita and Grandma in New Castle, Pennsylvania, learning to cook some of her most famous recipes and others, in hopes that I would end up with the "right" ones.

Although I learned a lot that week, I mostly learned that there is no "right" and "wrong" when it comes to food—even Grandma varied her recipes, depending on her mood or her guests. And, more importantly, I learned it doesn't really matter.

That's when it hit me. All recipes are based on, or are combinations of, what we've learned from our mothers and fathers, brothers and sisters, aunts and godmothers, grandmothers and grandfathers. We're all borrowers and learners and inventors. And, although some of us might be better at it than others, we each have one dish that we believe we can make better than anyone else.

After a few years of collecting recipes from both my parents families and in-laws, and with a lot of help from my mom, I've finally been able to pull them all together. And what I've ended up with is a family cookbook that goes well beyond what I had once considered to be the family classics. This book includes international dishes, such as Curt's Shopska Salad and Joe's Vegetarian Moussaka; new holiday favorites, like Debbie's Sweet Potato Soup for Thanksgiving, and older favorites like Judy's French Onion Soup for New Year's Day. I've received some delicious vegetarian dishes from Alexis and Janice (yes, including her Spanish Rice); some classic American dishes that came from Aunt Babs and my mom's grandmother; some traditional cookies from Carl and Anita, as well as my Gram's nutty fingers; some cooking tips from my father; a recipe from Roxanne that's sure to get me a proposal someday; some strange-sounding cocktails; and of course, all of the Christmas dinner recipes from Evelyn.

I have thoroughly enjoyed putting this book together and have particularly liked getting to know my family through their recipes. Each recipe, to me, tells a story—some of which I've included in the following pages and told in the voices of those who contributed. I hope you enjoy it as much as I have. So with that said, salute and mangia bene!

Kate DeVivo
Chicago, Illinois
August 2002

THE CHEFS

Joseph and Helen DeVivo (Grandma and Grandpa)
Janice DeVivo Aubrey Shoup (daughter)
Alexis Aubrey (Janice's daughter)
Roxanne Aubrey (Janice's daughter)
Mabel Aubrey (Janice's former mother-in-law)
Anita DeVivo (daughter)
Evelyn DeVivo Meine (daughter)
Curt Meine (Evelyn's son)
Kenny Meine (Evelyn's son)
Debbie Hoilman Meine (Evelyn's daughter-in-law,
Kenny's wife)
Glenn Meine (Evelyn's son)
Shelley Tainter Meine (Evelyn's daughter-in-law,
Glenn's wife)
Lee Meine (Evelyn's son)
Carl Meine (Lee and Sue's son)
Jody DeVivo (son)
Judy Pogue DeVivo (Grandma's daughter-in-law,
Jody's wife)
Joe DeVivo (Jody and Judy's son)
Rebecca DeVivo (Jody and Judy's daughter)

Kate DeVivo (Jody and Judy's daughter)
Babs and Bill Wells (Judy's aunt and uncle)
Jane Willey (Judy's aunt)
Peggy Pogue (Judy's mother)
G. G. Megee (Judy's grandmother)
Great Grandma DeMasi (Grandma's mother)
Stella Lombardo LoMonaco (Grandma's sister)
Ralphy Lombardo (Stella's son, Grandma's nephew)
Stella Suchy DeVivo (Alphonso DeVivo's wife,
Grandma's niece-in-law)
Rose DeVivo Rendulich (Grandma's niece)
Mrs. Sebastiani (I have no idea)

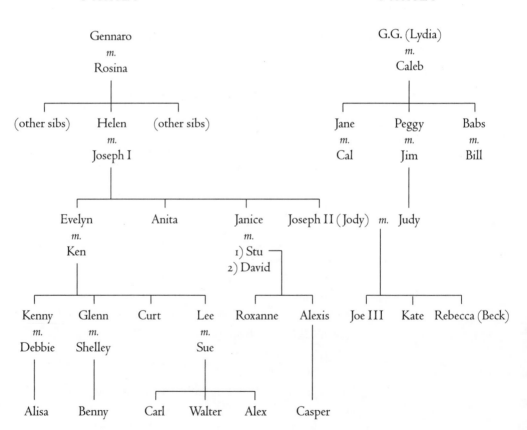

DeVivo/DeMasi Family   **Megee/Pogue Family**

Gennaro *m.* Rosina — G.G. (Lydia) *m.* Caleb

(other sibs) — Helen *m.* Joseph I — (other sibs) — Jane *m.* Cal — Peggy *m.* Jim — Babs *m.* Bill

Evelyn *m.* Ken — Anita — Janice *m.* 1) Stu 2) David — Joseph II (Jody) *m.* Judy

Kenny *m.* Debbie — Glenn *m.* Shelley — Curt — Lee *m.* Sue — Roxanne — Alexis — Joe III — Kate — Rebecca (Beck)

Alisa — Benny — Carl — Walter — Alex — Casper

ACKNOWLEDGMENTS

*T*hanks to all DeVivos, Meines, Shoups, Aubreys, Wells, Megees, and Pogues who took time out of their busy lives to e-mail, fax, mail, and recite over the phone recipes for this book. And to those of you who secretly gave me other peoples' recipes without their knowledge.

A special thanks to Anita and Grandma for hosting me in New Castle and teaching me some tricks of the trade for a week. I had a wonderful time and will never forget it.

Thanks to Anita DeVivo, Evelyn Meine, Doug Sohn, Greta Walters, and Chris Posdal for reading the manuscript and pointing out some glaring errors I would never have seen.

Thanks to my parents for encouraging me to do this, giving me good advice, and for funding the original family version.

And lastly, thanks to my mom, my favorite cook, who was my sous-chef on this project and without whom I never would have been able to finish this.

Mangia Bene!

Appetizers and Drinks

- Kate and Beck's Artichoke Dip
- Debbie's 4th of July Dip
- Judy's Deviled Eggs
- Kate's Bruschetta
- The Christmas Tradition: La Vigilia
- Judy's Cream Cheese Shrimp Appetizer
- Roxanne's Mussels Bella Vista
- Glenn and Shelley's Buffalo Wings: The official Silver Moon Blues Bar recipe
- The Blues Bar
- Evelyn's Antipasto with Celery-Olive Relish
- Great Grandmother DeMasi's Pinzimonio
- Debbie's Crab Cakes
- Evelyn's Deep-Fried Smelts
- Judy's Asparagus Rolls
- Janice's Sangria
- Roxanne's Margarita
- Beck's Skippers
- Curt's Own Made-Up Best Summer Drink Ever Concocted
- Jody's Martini

Kate and Beck's Artichoke Dip

2 14-ounce cans artichoke hearts,
  drained and chopped
1 cup grated Parmesan cheese
1 cup mayonnaise

3 cloves garlic, crushed
Splash Worcestershire sauce
Splash hot sauce
Chopped parsley for garnish

Combine everything but parsley. Put into 1-quart greased casserole. Bake at 350 degrees for 20 minutes. Garnish with parsley. Serve with toast points or crackers.

• Serves anyone who joins the DeVivos in Chicago on Christmas Eve

If you want to make the really good version, use extra garlic and cheese! —Beck

Debbie's 4th of July Dip

Taco seasoning mix to taste

1 8-ounce package cream cheese

½ head iceberg lettuce, finely
chopped

2 to 3 green onions, chopped

1 tomato, diced

½ small can sliced black olives

Finely shredded Cheddar cheese

Tortilla chips

Mix taco seasoning and cream cheese together. Spread on flat dinner-sized plate or pie tin. Layer next five ingredients in order listed. Serve with tortilla chips.

♦ *Serves* six to eight

Judy's Deviled Eggs

12 eggs

2 to 3 tablespoons mayonnaise

1 to 2 teaspoons yellow mustard

1 to 2 teaspoons sweet pickle relish

Salt and pepper to taste

$\frac{1}{2}$ to 1 teaspoon cider vinegar

Paprika for garnish

Hard boil eggs. Let cool. Peel and slice in half, lengthwise. Squeeze yolks into a bowl and mash up well with fork. Add mayonnaise, mustard, relish, salt, pepper, and vinegar until it tastes good. Stir until consistency is creamy. Spoon mixture into empty egg holes. Sprinkle tops lightly with paprika.

♦ *Makes* 24 deviled eggs

Kate's Bruschetta

It's hard to make this wrong or badly—it's also easy and fast if you have unexpected company or are always running late like me!   —Kate

French or Italian bread (or any other kind you find around your kitchen—can even be a little old!), about ½ foot to 1 foot long

3 to 5 fresh tomatoes, seeded and chopped into small bits (or 1 to 2 cans diced tomatoes)

Half handful fresh basil, cut small

1 to 2 teaspoons garlic, crushed

¼ to ½ red onion, diced

Any other herbs (fresh or dried) you want to add, such as oregano, parsley, or Italian seasoning to taste

A couple teaspoons or tablespoons olive oil

Splash of red wine vinegar

Shredded Parmesan or Romano cheese, to taste

Salt and pepper to taste

Cut bread diagonally into slices. (This will make you look like you know what you're doing.) Then, mix together all other ingredients, balancing amounts to taste, and spread over bread. You can also replace red onions with green ones or add green or red peppers. The most important thing is to mix everything in a bowl so that it looks like it's a salsa and is supposed to go together.

♦ *Serves* four to six

Glenn, Alexis, Joe, Debbie and the rest of the family take a breather at the end of one Christmas dinner at Jody and Judy's in Chicago.

THE CHRISTMAS TRADITION: LA VIGILIA

by Evelyn Meine

A tradition in the Italian family is the Christmas Eve supper, enjoyed in the hours before leaving the home where all have gathered before Midnight Mass. The centuries-old ritual of consuming only meatless dinners on this last evening before Christmas was known as La Vigilia, and the meal consisted of an odd number (usually five or seven) of courses using fish as the main ingredient. A typical DeVivo meal might consist of a shrimp appetizer, a cioppino (fish stew), a pasta course with clam or anchovy sauce, deep-fried smelts, and an oven-baked fish main course. To complete the meal, a side salad, vegetables (such as broccoli or cauliflower), and desserts leave the guests gasping for fresh air and needing to walk off the feast.

Here are some recipes that might be served during La Vigilia:

Judy's Cream Cheese Shrimp Appetizer

1 8-ounce package cream cheese
6 to 8 ounces shrimp
    cocktail sauce
½ pound small cooked shrimp
Crackers

Put cream cheese on plate. Spread shrimp sauce and shrimp over it. Spread both on cracker. Eat.

VARIATION

Substitute red or green pepper jelly for shrimp and shrimp cocktail sauce.

♦ *Serves* six to eight

Roxanne's Mussels Bella Vista

Bunch of mussels, about two dozen
7 to 8 cloves garlic
1 bunch flat parsley
3 to 4 lemons
Salt and pepper to taste

Clean and debeard mussels. Finely chop garlic and parsley. Squeeze lemons and add to garlic and parsley. Add salt and pepper to taste. The consistency should be a watery paste.

Steam the mussels in water. When they're done, arrange them on a plate and pour a spoonful of the garlic/parsley/lemon mix on each mussel. Can be served hot or cold. I like it cold. That way, the parsley has some texture as it tends to wilt if the mussels are too warm.

◆ *Serves* six to eight

Glenn and Shelley's Buffalo Wings

THE OFFICIAL SILVER MOON BLUES BAR RECIPE

2 pounds chicken wings
Oil for deep-frying
¼ pound butter
4 ounces hot sauce
Cider vinegar to taste

Garlic powder to taste
Blue cheese salad dressing
    for dipping
Celery stalks

Cut wings into "drums" and "paddles," discarding the tips. Deep-fry pieces till crispy. For sauce, mix butter and hot sauce. Cut the sauce with a little cider vinegar and add a little garlic powder. Dip the wings thoroughly in sauce and serve with blue cheese dressing and fresh cut celery.

♦ *Serves* six to eight, or ten to twelve, depending on how hungry people are

Glenn and Shelley's blues bar in Darien, Wisconsin

THE BLUES BAR

by Glenn Meine

The Silver Moon Blues Bar opened in late 1989 in a quiet corner of southern Wisconsin. People in this area love to eat great food, and roadhouses like the Silver Moon are famous for their home cooking. We felt it necessary to include the best recipes we could find, and where better to look than the family favorites? Although our wings are notable, it is the meatballs (see page 63 for Grandma's recipe), sausages, and coogootz (see page 119 for my mom's recipe) that bring attention to our heritage. There is no better feeling than to work in our establishment and smell these foods cooking. It is a way of giving our customers a sense of being at home. (Question often asked: Hey Glenn, do you have any of your mom's coogootz today?)

Evelyn's Antipasto with Celery-Olive Relish

ANTI (BEFORE) ... PASTO (PASTA)

Before there were heavy hors d'oeuvres or finger foods, there were antipasti. In my childhood, on very special occasions, like weddings, funerals, or holidays, the appearance of the antipasto on the table signaled the beginning of a special dinner. The kitchen artists had done it again. Masterpieces of color and design announced the start of another eating experience to be enjoyed by family and friends. Large platters of various munchies were carefully arranged so that one was almost afraid to disturb the pattern. The eyes said "no" but the stomach said "yes," and so the eating would begin.

The creative cook is limited only by his or her budget and storage space in the refrigerator when planning antipasto trays. Preparing the trays can be fun, but there are several groups of musts when eating this course.

—Evelyn

COLD CUTS

Prosciutto, sausages, salami, mortadella, ham, capicollo, and turkey

EGGS AND CHEESES

Deviled eggs, provolone, Asiago, Gorganzola, and mozzarella

FRUITS AND VEGETABLES

Cantaloupe, marinated eggplant, pickled peppers, mushrooms, artichoke hearts, fresh cauliflower and broccoli, tomatoes, celery, and fennel sticks

SEAFOOD

Anchovies, sardines, shrimp, tuna, mussels, squid, and clams

BASICS

Italian cured black and green olives, pickles, onions, breads, Italian rolls, and crackers

AND, OF COURSE

Olive oil and vinegar dressing, salt and pepper, and condiments

On a tray, lay out meats, cheeses, vegetables, and so on. To make Celery-Olive Relish, mix all ingredients listed below. Place relish in middle of tray and serve with bread and condiments.

Celery-Olive Relish

A small handful of inner leaves
  and heart of 1 stalk of celery,
  chopped
1½ cups green olives with
  pimentos, chopped coarsely
  (I break with fingers)

⅓ cup olive oil
Salt and coarse ground pepper
  to taste
2 or 3 garlic cloves, minced
Dash red or white wine vinegar
  (optional)

◆ *Servings* vary

Note: The amounts given for Celery-Olive Relish are very flexible and can be adjusted for personal taste.

Great Grandmother DeMasi's Pinzimonio

When Grandma's mother felt like snacking, she would often prepare pinzimonio. She would also serve it as a relish with a light meal. It's noisy, but nice.   —Anita

Celery
Salt and pepper
Olive oil

Clean celery and cut into 4- or 5-inch lengths. Mix salt, pepper, and olive oil to make a dip for the celery.

♦ *Servings* vary

Debbie's Crab Cakes

$\frac{1}{2}$ cup plain fresh (soft) bread
   crumbs
$\frac{1}{2}$ cup mayonnaise
1 egg
2 tablespoons lemon juice
1 tablespoon Worcestershire sauce
1 tablespoon Dijon mustard

2 green onions, thinly sliced
1 tablespoon chopped fresh
   parsley
1 teaspoon seafood seasoning
2 6$\frac{1}{2}$-ounce cans lump crabmeat,
   drained
2 tablespoons butter

Combine all the ingredients except the crabmeat and butter in bowl; mix well. Fold in the crabmeat, being careful not to break up the chunks. Form into sixteen equal-sized patties. Melt the butter in a large skillet over medium heat. Sauté patties in butter for 3 to 4 minutes per side, or until browned. Serve immediately.

◆ *Serves* sixteen, or eight with larger appetites

Evelyn's Deep-Fried Smelts

F resh smelts are not always available at Christmastime, but frozen smelts, often already battered, usually are. If you can find fresh smelts, prepare them for deep-frying by cutting off the head, then splitting and gutting them. The bones and tails are soft and need not be removed. Wash them in cold water and dry them off.   —Evelyn

Kenny, sometime in the late 1970s, shows off a nicely fried smelt.

"The smelt is a delicate, translucent fish measuring four to seven inches in length. It is rich, oily and mild flavored. There are many varieties, including the rainbow smelt, found along the Atlantic Coast, and the whitebait smelt, found on the Pacific Coast. The euchalon smelt, also known as the candlefish, got its nickname because Native Americans would dry these high-fat fish, run a wick through them and use them as candles. Fresh smelt are best from September through May."

—From the *Food Lover's Companion*, third edition, by Sharon Tyler Herbst. Published in 2001 by Barron's Educational Series, Inc.

DRY INGREDIENTS (COATING)

1 cup white or yellow cornmeal

1 cup flour

1 tablespoon cornstarch

¼ teaspoon garlic powder

1 teaspoon baking powder

LIQUID INGREDIENTS

1 egg

1 cup milk

1 cup water

This recipe can be used for about 50 smelts.

For heavier batter, mix dry ingredients. Mix liquid ingredients in separate bowl and add to dry mix. Let stand 15 to 20 minutes. Add more liquid, if needed.

For lighter batter, keep ingredients separate. Dip smelt into dry coating, then into liquid ingredients, then into coating again.

To deep-fry: Heat oil to between 350 degrees and 375 degrees, until a cube of day-old bread browns in 1 minute. Drop battered smelts into oil, a few at a time, until they are browned on all sides, moist, and easily flaked. Drain on paper towels. Do not overcook!

◆ Serves six to eight

Note: The smelts, though delicious, are lethal when it comes to fryers. One year I tried making Gloves (see recipe, p. 185) with the smelts fryer and they stank. Literally.   —Kate

KENNY'S VARIATION

Mix 1 cup flour with salt, coarse pepper, and garlic powder to taste in paper bag (no plastic allowed). Dip smelts in milk, then roll them around in the paper bag to coat. Place battered smelts in deep fryer or skillet in which you have oil as hot as you can get it. As smelts float and bubble and boil, turn them over at least once. Smelts only take a minute or two to cook, unless they are really big. When they are done, lift out with a slotted spoon and place on paper towels to drain the oil. Give them another sprinkle of salt, and serve!

Judy's Asparagus Rolls

I originally got this recipe from my friend Barbara Clary. Beck and I have made it a few times, and it's always a hit!   —Judy

16 white bread slices

1 8-ounce cream cheese package,
   softened

4 ounces blue cheese, crumbled

1 to 2 15-ounce cans asparagus,
   drained

½ stick melted butter

Remove crusts from bread and flatten bread with rolling pin. Combine cream cheese and blue cheese in bowl. Spread on bread pieces to cover and add one or two pieces asparagus per slice of bread. Roll up each slice of bread and then cut into thirds. Cover with melted butter. Bake on cookie sheet at 375 degrees for 20 to 25 minutes until golden brown.

♦ *Makes* four dozen rolls

Note: To make ahead, freeze rolls on cookie sheet and put frozen rolls into plastic bag to store until you're ready to use them.

Janice's Sangria

1 large banana

1 large navel orange

1 large lemon, sliced thin

2 quarts Burgundy wine

½ cup sugar

1 quart soda water

Slice banana into a large glass pitcher. Add peel of orange. Squeeze orange juice into pitcher. Add lemon, wine, and sugar. Chill 3 hours. Add soda and serve immediately.

◆ *Serves* four

Roxanne's Margarita

I got this recipe from my dad, Stu—an affable guy who knows how to make a mean cocktail.   —Roxanne

Good tequila

Triple Sec

Fresh squeezed lemon juice

Mix 2 parts tequila, 2 parts Triple Sec, and 1 part lemon juice. The secret is to freeze this stuff for at least 24 hours—guaranteed to get rid of the heartburn factor. DO NOT USE LIME. Serve over ice.

◆ *Serves* any number of people, depending on the size of the "parts" you choose

Warning: This stuff is lethal. Do not try to operate heavy machinery after consuming. Three 4-ounce glasses will sufficiently inebriate anybody.

TOMMY'S VARIATION

Before serving, add an egg white to mixture and whip it up in a blender. That will give it a soft froth.

Beck's Skippers

This recipe is borrowed from Christina Welter, a Minnesota native. To me, that explains a lot. Especially considering the only other Minnesotan I know holds Jagermeister and blackberry brandy as two of her favorite drinks.   —Beck

1 12-ounce can condensed
    lemonade mix
Vodka equal to can of
    lemonade mix
2 12-ounce cans cheap beer

Pour the can of lemonade stuff into a bowl or pitcher. Refill the can with vodka and add to lemonade stuff. Add beer, stir, and chill. It sounds gross, but is very tasty.

◆ *Serves* two to eight, depending on how much you want yourself

Curt's Own Made-Up
Best Summer Drink Ever Concocted

Absolut Kurant
   (Black Currant) vodka
Lemonade
Ice

Not much to it. Yellow lemonade seems to work better than pink. The standard ratio (I'm still experimenting vigorously) is about 80% lemonade to 20% vodka. That's for taste. A little more on the vodka end, obviously, if you want (or you want to deliver) a stronger kick. Salut!

◆ *Servings* vary

Jody's Martini

First of all, I don't recognize such a thing as a vodka martini. There is only a gin martini. Period. Also, I don't like the other bastardizations of the martini. All the different fruits you put in it, the vermouth options, the cutesy names. I simply don't understand why anyone wants to screw up a perfect drink.

Speaking of perfect, the drink called "the Perfect Martini" is 4 parts gin, 1 part dry vermouth. That's how they drank it in the old days. It's horrible. Too sour with all that vermouth.

The present-day "Dry Martini" is just a squirt of vermouth in a bunch of gin. If you like it really dry, you make it a really small squirt, maybe just a drop. That's pretty much how I make a martini. Nothing magic about it. Lots of ice, enough gin for a drink, a drop or two of vermouth. I prefer to put this in a shaker, shake it, and pour it into an ice-cold high-stem martini glass. And I prefer a twist of lemon peel in my martini, as opposed to an olive. But at

Jody's Martini

home, I usually drink it on the rocks with no fruit. I did have a martini once at Chasens in L.A. that was made with a twist of orange peel. It was fantastic.   —Jody

Gin

Vermouth

◆ *Servings* vary

Soups

- Wedding Soup
- La Famiglia
- Judy's Gazpacho
- Debbie's Sweet Potato Soup
- The Story of the Three Turkeys
- Judy's French Onion Soup
- Evelyn's Cioppino
- Babs and Bill's Succotash
- Grandma's Vegetable Soup with Sausage
- Evelyn's Minestrone
- Judy's Split Pea Soup
- Joe's Venison Chili

Wedding Soup

Growing up in an Italian American community provided me with many experiences that could not be learned in any other way but living them day in and day out in a loving household. Special memories of holiday dinners, weddings, baptisms, confirmations, and out-of-town guests accompany this traditional soup. There are shortcuts that reduce the preparation time for this delicacy, but every work of art takes time and attention—and to partake in a healthy serving of "made from scratch" wedding soup is to hear the opening movement of a Beethoven symphony or to enjoy the first act of a Shakespeare play. —Evelyn

I-Chicken Broth

1 4- to 5-pound stewing chicken, washed and cleaned

4 outer stalks celery

4 medium whole carrots

2 medium whole onions

5 quarts salted water

Place whole chicken in water and bring to boil. As water boils, remove scum that forms on surface. Add vegetables and cook together until meat begins to fall from bones. Remove chicken and vegetables and strain broth.

I usually remove the first batch of vegetables and strain broth in case there are little pieces of bone. If the veggies are too soft, I dice a whole bunch more and replace. —Evelyn

II-Vegetables

Cooked vegetables (from above)

Celery leaves, minced

2 to 4 pounds escarole, washed thoroughly and cut into bite-sized pieces

If strained vegetables are firm, dice and add to broth. If firmer vegetables are preferred, fresh vegetables can replace cooked ones and be added to the broth. Meanwhile, core and separate escarole leaves before washing. Save tender center of escarole for salad. Add 2 cups water to deep kettle and cook chopped escarole until leaves are limp and spines smash between fingers. Cool; drain and set aside.

III-Meatballs

½ to 1 pound ground beef	2 teaspoons minced parsley
3 eggs	2 small cloves garlic, minced
1 cup bread crumbs	Salt and pepper to taste
3 tablespoons grated Parmesan cheese	

Mix above ingredients well. Mixture should be firm enough to be shaped into small balls, each the size of a hazelnut. Make meatballs and fry in oil until lightly browned, or place on a greased cookie sheet to bake in oven at 400 degrees, until lightly browned.

Line up small-sized meatballs and bake until lightly browned.

IV-Finale

4 to 6 hardboiled eggs, cooled, cut
   into medium-sized pieces

Separate chicken meat from bones, gristle, and fat. Sliver meat into bite-sized pieces. Add diced vegetables, escarole, meatballs, chicken pieces, and eggs to broth and continue simmering for about an hour. Serve with croutons.

VARIATION

Add small pasta, like acini di pepe, to finished soup.

◆ *Serves* eight to twelve, depending on size of serving

My mother never made soup. It came in style when they began making big dinners for weddings. I made soup on any holiday. And I don't know what else to put in it except greens. I cut them small—the escarole—like the size of the tip of your finger. I hate it when the chicken in the soup hangs down over the spoon and the soup drips onto your face. When pieces are small, you eat the whole thing. Cut all the vegetables the same size . . . it'll look real nice. —Grandma

LA FAMIGLIA

by Jody DeVivo

According to family legend, my father, Joe, fell in love with my mother, Helen DeMasi, when they were teenagers going to choir practice at St. Lucy's church in New Castle, Pennsylvania. At that time, my father was a stutterer. And my mother had something called Bell's palsy, which made her mouth look lopsided. Obviously, they were made for each other. To shorten a long and complicated story—involving a school for stutterers in Indianapolis, the Depression, winemaking, lots of food, and my grandmother's distrust of musicians—my father overcame his stuttering and my grandmother's objections, my mother's mouth straightened up, and they got married. And stayed that way for almost seventy years.

My father had come to this country from Italy in 1912 when he was nine years old. He got a job with the B&O Railroad when he was fourteen and worked for them for fifty

This is an excerpt from my father's book *Bands!* which is a memoir of growing up in the '50s as an untalented musician in a very musical, Italian-American town.   —Kate

years. He also moonlighted at odd jobs, like selling Electrolux vacuum cleaners door-to-door and hanging wallpaper. But his life was the church and music. He taught himself to play trumpet and other brass instruments. He played guitar and mandolin at parties and family gatherings. He sang in church choirs and eventually became the choir director at St. Mary's, the largest Catholic church in town.

My mother was born in this country, but she just made it—she has older siblings who were born in Italy. She always had an impressive, hard-to-please intellect, and I'm positive she had the ability to manage a giant corporation. But like most women of her time, she had to be satisfied with managing her husband, and becoming a terrific cook and mother.

Once my mother got her man, she was never heard to sing again.

Judy's Gazpacho

1 green bell pepper, halved
   and seeded
1 cucumber, peeled and halved
3 cups low-sodium tomato juice
1 onion, halved
2 garlic cloves, peeled

$\frac{1}{8}$ teaspoon hot red pepper sauce
$\frac{1}{4}$ cup red wine vinegar
2 tomatoes, chopped
4 green onions, thinly sliced
$\frac{1}{2}$ cup seasoned croutons

Purée all but the last two ingredients. Chill before serving. Serve garnished with green onions and croutons.

♦ *Serves* six

Debbie's Sweet Potato Soup

3 tablespoons butter

1 medium onion, coarsely chopped

1 teaspoon curry powder

9 cups chicken stock

5 to 6 medium sweet potatoes, peeled and cubed

¼ cup maple syrup

2 to 3 sprigs fresh thyme

Pinch of cayenne pepper

1 cup cream

⅛ teaspoon freshly grated nutmeg

Salt and white pepper to taste

Melt butter over medium heat in a large saucepan. Add the onion and curry powder and cook for 5 or 6 minutes, stirring occasionally, until onion is soft.

Meanwhile, bring chicken stock to a simmer in a separate saucepan.

Add sweet potatoes to onion, then add stock, maple syrup, thyme, and cayenne pepper. Simmer, partially covered, for about 25 minutes, or until the sweet potatoes are soft.

Remove the thyme sprigs and puree soup in batches. Strain pureed soup, if desired, and return to the pan. Add cream, nutmeg, salt and pepper to taste, and heat to serving temperature.

• *Serves* twelve to fourteen

THE STORY OF THE THREE TURKEYS

by Jody DeVivo

Once upon a time, Evelyn gave each member of her family a check for $25 and asked us to donate them to someone in need. This is the story of how we found someone in need because of our three Thanksgiving turkeys.

We really only wanted one turkey. And for a while, that's all we had. Judy bought it way ahead of time, and we kept it in the freezer until a few days before Thanksgiving. Then I moved it to our basement refrigerator, so it could thaw slowly. Unfortunately, I had forgotten that there's a place in that refrigerator where, if you set something frozen on it, it stays frozen.

So, on Thanksgiving day, Judy and I got up early to work on the bird so it would be ready for dinner. (Becky had brought two friends home with her from college. Joe and Kate were home. And our friends Mike and Jean Malatak were coming, so we were going to have nine people for dinner.)

I brought the turkey upstairs, we unwrapped it, and lo

Text reprinted from *The Mama DeVivo Newsletter*, Issue 23, December 5, 1995.

and behold, the top had thawed, but the bottom was still frozen solid. It was a rock. You could have cracked nuts with it. You could have hammered nails with it. It was real hard.

Before Judy could panic, I said, "Don't panic, dear. I shall go out and get us a fresh turkey, one that isn't frozen." And Judy, fighting back tears, said, "Oh, I do hope you can find one, dear. We have nine for dinner, you know." (In crisis situations, Judy and I tend to talk like Ozzie and Harriet.)

I tore out of the house, hopped into the minivan, and drove straight to the grocery store. It was around 8 A.M., but they were open. I went directly to the meat department and asked the Meat Man if they had any fresh, not frozen, turkeys. He pointed to the cooler next to me and said, "right there." I looked down and saw a flock of turkeys lined up like bathing beauties on a sunny beach. And their tags all said "fresh, not frozen." I quickly grabbed a 20-pounder, shot through the express lane, and whisked the bird home. (Actually, I drove the bird home instead of whisking it home. Whisk brooms are so small, it would have taken me forever.)

I should have taken the time and had a closer look at the turkey. Because when we unwrapped it, we discovered Mr. Smarty Pants Meat Man was wrong, the label had lied, the bird was frozen solid. You could have dented a car with it. You could have pulverized stones with it. You could have shot it from a cannon and done big damage to the enemy. It was real hard.

Turkeys, turkeys all around, but nary a bite to eat. In just a few hours, we were going to have nine people at our house expecting a real Thanksgiving dinner. Judy was starting to twitch. Something had to be done fast. So I went to another grocery store.

This time I conducted an autopsy on the fresh-not-frozen bird I found there. I flapped its wings. I wiggled its legs. I poked it in the belly. And it flapped and wiggled and poked like a true thawed turkey. So I bought it, feeling a little déjà vuish, and when I got it home, Judy pronounced Turkey #3

stuffable, cookable, bastable, and potentially very edible. So the crisis was over, the problem was solved, and Thanksgiving was thankable once again.

Except we had all those turkeys. What should we do with all those turkeys?

Well, this is what we decided. We'd cook and eat #3. Turkey #2 was still frozen, so we could keep it in the freezer for a Christmas meal. Turkey #1 was half thawed, and we couldn't refreeze it. So I called our old neighbor, Germaine, who often works in a soup kitchen for St. Vincent DePaul. I told her about our turkey and asked if they could use it. She said, "They certainly can! Four hundred homeless people are coming to the soup kitchen tomorrow, so I'll be over to pick it up in the morning." And that took care of all the turkeys.

Except it didn't. Turkey #3 was delicious. Turkey #2 was still frozen. But the next morning, Germaine didn't show up for Turkey #1. So I called her, thinking she forgot, and found out that St. Vincent DePaul's kitchen had caught fire on Thanksgiving Day and the stove and steam table had burned up. So before she could pick up the turkey and prepare any food, Germaine had to go out and buy new equipment.

Well, to make a long story short, Judy, Becky, and I gave her our $25 checks from Evelyn. And I gave a little extra besides. And we gave her Turkey #1, too, which was probably thawed by then. And other people donated money and food too. So those 400 people had a good dinner.

And that's the story of the three turkeys.

Judy's French Onion Soup

This is the way our family starts our New Year's Day meal. I don't know why I started making it or where I got it. I was looking for some kind of soup to go with the rest of the meal that I grew up with and have been making it now for thirty years.   —Judy

4 tablespoons butter

2 tablespoons olive oil

7 cups sliced onions

1 teaspoon salt

3 tablespoons flour

2 quarts beef stock, hot

Croutons (see below)

Melt butter and oil. Add onions; cook 20 to 30 minutes, until golden brown. Sprinkle salt and flour over onions and cook, stirring, 2 to 3 minutes. Add hot stock. Simmer partially covered 30 to 40 minutes.

Serve croutons separately.

Croutons

Cut crusts off of any sliced bread you choose. Place the bread in 350-degree oven for 10 minutes, coat with oil, and turn. Cook 10 more minutes.

◆ Serves eight to ten

◆

Judy's New Year's Day Menu

French Onion Soup   39

Roast Pork   106

Sauerkraut   145

Mashed Potatoes

Green Vegetable

Waldorf Salad   168

Rolls and Butter

Cookies (see Desserts,

page 181, for a recipe)

◆ ◆ ◆

Evelyn's Cioppino

I didn't grow up with cioppino. We had cod soup—the same thing, but with only cod.   —Evelyn

3 onions, chopped

3 cloves garlic, chopped fine

½ cup olive oil

½ cup Italian parsley, chopped fine

1 28-ounce can stewed tomatoes, coarsely chopped

2 tablespoons lemon juice

4½ cups water

1½ teaspoons salt

2 cups chicken broth

1 green pepper, seeded and chopped

¼ teaspoon each: dried thyme, basil, and oregano

½ teaspoon each: paprika and coarse black pepper

1 large bay leaf

3 to 5 pounds fish and shellfish (snapper, mussels, scallops, medium shrimp, not cod)

2 cups white wine

1. In a big pot, lightly brown onions and garlic in oil.

2. Add all other ingredients, except fish and wine.

3. Adjust spices to your taste.

4. Cover and simmer for about 30 minutes before adding fish.

5. Bring to boil; add fish.

6. Reduce heat, add wine, and simmer for another 25 to 30 minutes.

Optional: Throw in all your leftover hot sauces, Bloody Mary mix, tomato juice, and so on. Add a little sugar, if sauce is too tart. Sometimes I add more chicken broth to make it more soupy.   —Evelyn

♦ *Serves* **twelve**

Babs and Bill's Succotash

1 ½ pounds fresh lima beans
   (the big ones, not baby limas)
Salt and pepper to taste
4 to 5 ears fresh white sweet corn
   (e.g., Silver Queen), cut from
   cob

¼ cup butter
Milk
Biscuits or rolls

Cook beans. When boiling, add salt and pepper to water. When beans are almost done, add corn and continue cooking until beans are tender, but not mushy.

Turn off heat. Add butter. Add as much milk as you need to make a soup. Reheat, but **DO NOT BOIL**. Move off burner so succotash doesn't over-cook. Serve with biscuits or rolls.

◆ *Serves* four to six

Grandma's Vegetable Soup with Sausage

2 pounds Italian sausage

2 medium onions, finely chopped

2 garlic cloves, minced

4 carrots, peeled and diced

4 small zucchini (about 1 pound), diced

2 green bell peppers, seeded and diced

10 cups chicken broth, preferably low salt

2 28-ounce cans crushed tomatoes in tomato puree

2 teaspoons dried basil, crumbled

1 teaspoon dried oregano, crumbled

1 cup uncooked orzo (rice-shaped pasta)

Salt and freshly ground pepper to taste

1¼ cups freshly grated Parmesan cheese

Remove casings from the sausage and discard. Brown sausage in a heavy Dutch oven or large saucepan, mashing it with the back of a spoon until the meat is no longer pink and has rendered most of its fat.

Spoon out most of the fat from the cooked sausage and discard. Add onions and garlic and cook, stirring until soft but not browned. Add carrots, zucchini, bell peppers, chicken broth, tomatoes, basil, and oregano and bring to a boil. When the soup is boiling, add orzo and cook for 20 minutes more. Season to taste with salt and pepper. Serve in heavy soup bowls. Sprinkle Parmesan cheese over each serving.

Like most hearty soups, this tastes best if it is cooled, refrigerated overnight, then reheated to serve. It may also be frozen.

◆ Serves twelve to sixteen

Evelyn's Minestrone

2 to 3 pounds beef bone or
   ham bone

6 carrots, diced

½ head cabbage, chopped

1 28- to 30-ounce can tomatoes,
   broken up with fingers

2 to 4 potatoes, diced

2 onions, chopped

2 cloves garlic, minced

3 slices bacon

½ teaspoon each dried rosemary,
   basil, and parsley

2 beef bouillon cubes

½ pound uncooked small pasta,
   such as ditalini

1 16-ounce can red kidney beans

1 cup red wine

¼ cup olive oil

4 or 5 stalks celery, diced

Salt and pepper to taste

Bay leaf (optional)

Simmer meat bone in 2 gallons water for 1½ hours. Add carrots and cabbage. When carrots are almost tender, add tomatoes and potatoes.

Sauté onions and garlic with bacon and add to soup with all other ingredients. Simmer 25 to 30 minutes. Adjust seasonings to your preference.

◆ *Serves* twelve or more

Judy's Split Pea Soup

2 cups dry split peas

3 quarts water

1 ham bone (optional)

2 teaspoons salt

½ teaspoon pepper

¼ teaspoon dried marjoram

1½ cups chopped onions

¾ cup chopped carrots

¾ cup chopped celery

Combine peas and water. Bring to a boil and let cook 2 minutes. Remove from heat. Cover and let stand 1 hour.

Add ham bone, salt, pepper, marjoram, and onions. Cover and simmer 1½ hours.

Add carrots and celery. Continue simmering until tender.

♦ *Serves* ten to twelve

Joe's Venison Chili

This won chili of the year at the University of Georgia Institute of Ecology's annual chili cook-off in 1995.

About 2 pounds fresh venison and
  beef roast, cubed
¼ to ½ cup olive oil
1 large onion, chopped
1 green pepper, seeded and
  chopped
1 red pepper, seeded and chopped
3 stalks celery, chopped
1 32-ounce can peeled whole
  tomatoes
1 46-ounce can spicy tomato juice
1 32-ounce can chili beans
Beans from one of those 15-bean
  soup mixes, soaked overnight
  so they are properly mushy

1 15-ounce can kidney beans
A bunch of fresh jalapenos, seeded
  and chopped (if you've got a
  habanero handy, use it)
1 12-ounce can tomato paste
Black pepper
1 teaspoon hot chili pepper
1 bottle home-brewed stout
  or porter*
Any other sauces you might have
  lying around the kitchen that
  need to be used (steak sauce,
  Bloody Mary mix, pasta sauce,
  hot sauce, ketchup, BBQ sauce)

1. Brown meat in oil.

2. Add onion and cook until limp.

3. Add everything else.

4. Simmer and stir for 18 hours. (This is not a joke. My roommate and I took turns waking up the night before the competition.)

♦ *Serves* twenty

Note: I home-brew my own beer. Substitute another fine beer if you must.

Pizzas and Pastas

- Grandma's Pizza
- New Castle, Pennsylvania
- Keneve's: Evelyn and Ken's Pizza Shop
- Evelyn's Pizza
- CSO Radiothon Pizza Party
- Evelyn's Stuffed Greens Pizza
- Joe's Stuffed Manicotti
- Grandma's Spaghetti and Meatballs
- Sauce Thoughts from Grandma
- Evelyn's Pasta Sauce
- Grandma's Pasta Fazool
- Pavarotti and Pasta Fazool
- Alexis's Pasta Fazool
- Evelyn's Pasta with Clam Sauce
- Grandma's Pasta Alberto
- Homemade Pasta, Grandma Style
- Grandma's Oily-Oilies
- Kate's Vodka Pasta

Grandma's Pizza

Grandma demonstrated this recipe to cousin Rose one 4th of July, and Anita wrote down the procedure as Grandma worked. Some of Grandma's comments are included in the procedure.

Dough

1 pack rapid-rise yeast

¼ cup lukewarm water

1 teaspoon sugar

3 cups flour

1 teaspoon or less salt

1 tablespoon sugar

2 tablespoons olive oil

1 cup water

Sauce

1 clove garlic

1½ tablespoons vegetable oil

1 8-ounce can tomato sauce (may add a chopped fresh or frozen tomato)

1 teaspoon sugar

Salt, pepper, oregano, and basil (dried) to taste

Other

Romano cheese, grated

Oil for drizzling

Mozzarella or mild provolone cheese, shredded

Note about cheese: Grandma uses small amounts, which makes this pizza very light. However, amounts can be adjusted to chef's taste!

Y'oonz should spread sauce evenly with fork like Grandma.

First assemble all ingredients, bowls, and pans. Preheat oven to midway between 325 degrees and 350 degrees.

TO MAKE DOUGH

In a small bowl, stir rapid-rise yeast into ¼ cup lukewarm water. Add 1 teaspoon sugar and set aside. Put flour in mixing bowl and make a well in flour. Add salt, sugar, and oil. When the yeast and water foam, add to the flour, using 1 cup water to clean out any remaining yeast. Mix with a spatula. As you mix, clean the sides of the bowl. When the dough is well mixed, you can turn it by spatula or by hand. If you knead it by hand, pour a little oil into a small container and oil your fingers as needed to keep dough from sticking to them. Knead the dough until it's smooth and forms a ball, just a minute or two. Surface of dough should be oily. Level the dough in the bowl, cover it, and let it rest in a warm place until the sauce is ready.

TO MAKE SAUCE

Chop garlic. Lightly brown in oil. (Optional: If using frozen or fresh tomatoes, peel, chop, and add to garlic. Break up the pieces with a fork and cook off the water.) Add tomato sauce, sugar, salt, pepper, oregano, and basil to taste. Cook until thick, not watery. Cool before using. This should be enough for a large pizza.

Grease 12×18-inch cookie sheet with shortening. (If you use a smaller pan, pizza will be thick and high.) Turn out dough in center of pan. Stretch it in both directions. Then, working from the center, pat evenly to fill the pan. Top with the sauce, spreading it around with a fork. Add grated Romano cheese and oregano. Drizzle with oil. Set pizza aside for about 15 minutes, or until dough rises to rim of pan. The more it rises, the lighter the crust.

Bake for 20 minutes or more. Lay out a wire rack for cooling when pizza is done, to keep it from steaming. Check the bottom of the crust for even browning. Just before removing pizza from oven, top with shredded mozzarella or provolone cheese and leave in the oven just long enough to melt the cheese. Transfer the pizza to the wire rack to cool. Cut pieces with scissors.

♦ *Makes* one large pizza

New Castle, Pennsylvania

by Jody DeVivo

When somebody names something as big as a town, you'd think they'd be so proud of the responsibility they'd use a little creativity—it's not every day you get to name a town. But, from the looks of it, people are more proud of where they've been than where they are. Maybe it makes a little sense that there are Moscows, Londons, Romes, and Pragues all over the United States; they're names of world capitals. But New Castles? My computer's mapping program shows twenty-six of them sprinkled all over the country. That's not even counting the counties. Or the New Castles in other countries. (I have a picture of my wife standing in front of a sign in Italy that welcomes you to, you guessed it, Nuovocastello!)

I had always assumed that New Castle, Pennsylvania, was named after Newcastle, England. But John Carlyle Stewart, who laid out the town way back in 1798, named it after his hometown, New Castle, *Delaware*. Since that New

This is an excerpt from my father's book, *Bands!* —Kate

Castle in Delaware was named after Newcastle, England, we're talking here of a third-generation New Castle.

I never appreciated the hills of New Castle until I moved away to live in the flatness of Illinois. Although I eventually learned to love the minimalist beauty of the big sky and straight-line horizon of the Midwest, to this day I miss the ups and downs of Western Pennsylvania.

You'll find New Castle 50 miles north of Pittsburgh and 20 miles east of Youngstown, Ohio. Many people know it as the first exit on the Pennsylvania Turnpike going east, or as the last exit going west.

Comfortably nestled in a valley with big hills on its north side and rivers to the south, New Castle has old iron bridges, large parks with waterfalls, and several grand mansions. But most people live in modest two- or three-bedroom homes that they decorate for the holidays. They put friendship candles in their windows and have vegetable gardens. Lawns are well watered and neatly manicured, and you'll see the occasional Madonna. And folks from the New Castles all over the world are really tired of hearing jokes about hauling coals back to it.

About half the people in New Castle are of Italian descent, mostly from the same part of Italy, the province of Caserta, a little north of Naples. The other half is made up of everything else. There are Jews, Syrians, Lebanese, Greeks, Poles, Blacks, Irish, and even a few White Anglo Saxies. And there are also the black-suited Amish, living just north of town, horse-and-buggying down Route 18, bringing their eggs and cheese and hard labor into town to sell.

For all that diversity, as I grew up, people generally got along with each other. We went to the same high school, played in the same bands and ball teams, shopped in the same stores. We also went to each others' parties and picnics and ate each others' wonderful foods and danced to each others' music. We seemed to enjoy our differences more than people do in most places.

I'm sure there was plenty of prejudice floating around, but most of it floated above my head or beyond my eyesight. Actually, the most blatant bigotry I witnessed as I was growing up was directed at Italians by other Italians. Everybody knew the Bruzzese (Italians from Abruzzi) were capotost' (hard heads), i.e., stubborn. And the Calabrese (Italians from Calabria) were known to be very crafty. I never found out what the Casertans were known for, but I doubt that the Bruzzese and the Calabrese thought we were perfect.

New Castle has had its brushes with fame over the years. The Warner Brothers opened their first movie house there. Shenango Pottery was the country's biggest maker of china, and its logo can still be found under cups and plates all over the world, including several sets of White House china. A high school classmate of mine, Walter Mangham, held the United States high school record in the high jump for many years. New Castle's Chuck Tanner was the manager of the Pittsburgh Pirates in '79 when they won the World Series. (He now has a restaurant a half block from my mother's old house.) And many of the fireworks that exploded all over the country to welcome in the new millennium, and the ones that lit up the skies of New York City to celebrate the Statue of Liberty's big birthday bash—they came from New Castle.

KENEVE'S:
EVELYN AND KEN'S PIZZA SHOP

as told to Kate DeVivo by Evelyn Meine

We were married in 1950, when I was twenty-four. Ken's father was a European-born commercial grower and owned a greenhouse with his two sons, which he left to us when he retired. Originally it was a floral greenhouse, but the last years were devoted to growing tomatoes. We would deliver tomatoes to Pittsburgh, and after a while it seemed a good idea to also sell them at our own outdoor market. So Ken would go to Pittsburgh, deliver our tomatoes, and then would buy produce to sell at our market. We did that for two summers, but were faced with the need to produce income through the winter months, especially when Ken decided to finish his education. By this time I was in my early thirties and had three sons. In a town like New Castle, with a high population of Italian Americans who appreciated good food, we decided to open Keneve's pizza shop. It was located across from a busy shopping center, and we soon found out that many folks other than Italians loved pizza—especially Keneve's pizza.

Uncle Steve loaned me $250 for a used oven, pots, pans, and enough groceries to produce a limited menu. And I had a carpenter friend who helped me build things in the shop. Ken would go to college during the day and come home and work the shop at night with me. I also worked every day in a doctor's office, so I hired two women to prep the food while I was away, and they ran a little lunchtime business. Grandma and Grandpa DeVivo would also come in and help them out, and other times they would baby-sit our children, by that time totaling four boys.

The pizza was our own, based on Grandma's recipe. Grandma never made prebaked crusts, though. Ken had observed several shops and found a couple that were doing prebaked crusts, so we developed that, too. We always used the best ingredients—we were never chintzy. For a week, we had "tastings," where we would invite people in to get some feedback (no pun intended). We always used provolone instead of mozzarella, and we made our own sausage. When we started the business we became acquainted with a fellow who sold a tasty pizza sauce wholesale. We used his pizza sauce as our base and added certain ingredients to make it our own. Eventually we didn't buy his sauce anymore and made it all from scratch. No one ever knew how we mixed it. Only when we sold the shop did we tell the new owners how we made our secret sauce. The following recipe is pretty much it.

It was a small place. A counter—no tables—only four stools, and TV trays, for those who could sit on the few other chairs we had. It was mostly a take-out business. People would call in, and by the time they made it down to the shop, their pizza was ready. But sometimes people wouldn't bother calling in, because they wanted to hang around and see who was there—it became a gathering spot. We had a fireplace, and we would hang art by local artists, even if it was only a few pieces. A good night for us was if we sold fifty to seventy-five pizzas. That's a weekend night. There were other nights that

we would sell maybe twenty. It wasn't a lot, but the profit on pizza is very high, because the cost of ingredients is very low.

We also served sandwiches, almost as much as we served pizza. Meatball sandwiches, subs, you name it. People would come in and make up their own. Cousin Ralphy would come in with two or three of his friends from local colleges. And they would invent new sandwiches. We had a rule—if someone created and ate the sandwich more than three times, then we'd put that sandwich on the board. Ralphy invented one sandwich, which included everything but the kitchen sink. He called it "The Tumor"—because when he ate it he always wanted two more.

It was a hard time for us then and it was a lot of work. Since Ken was a musician and in college, sometimes he would have concerts to play and come in right after and serve customers with his tux on. But the profit in the long run was pretty good. We earned enough to keep us all going, and our kids got to eat pizza for breakfast. We had the business for five or six years before we sold it and moved to Detroit. It was hard work, but we had a lot of fun.

Evelyn's Pizza

Dough

1 tablespoon sugar

⅝ cup warm water (110° to 115°F)

2 packages dry yeast

4 cups flour

⅛ cup oil

½ teaspoon salt

In a small bowl, mix sugar, water, and yeast together and let sit till it begins to foam. Meanwhile, measure flour into a mixing bowl. Make a well in the center of the flour and add the oil, salt, and liquid yeast mixture. Slowly mix the flour and liquids together until dough is smooth. If needed, add more flour slowly until the dough is smooth and pliable. Knead for a few moments, then coat the dough ball with oil and place in a bowl. Cover with a dish towel and let stand in warm place (about 80°) until dough has doubled.

After it has doubled in bulk, punch down the dough until all air bubbles have burst. Turn out the dough and divide into four equal pieces. Stretch to fit greased cookie sheets or 12-inch round pans; spray or spread a light coat of oil over dough and allow to rise again for about ½ hour, or until doubled.

Sauce

3 tablespoons olive oil

1 large onion, chopped

2 cloves garlic, chopped

1 small green pepper, seeded and
   chopped

2 28- to 30-ounce cans crushed
   tomatoes

1 teaspoon each oregano, basil
   (dried)

1 teaspoon sugar

Salt and pepper

While dough is rising, heat oil in a deep skillet. Add onion, garlic, and green pepper. Cook together until limp. Then add crushed tomatoes and cook together for 10 minutes. Add seasonings and adjust to taste. Cook until thickened. Allow to cool.

When dough is ready and sauce has cooled, carefully spoon sauce over risen dough. Be careful to not puncture the dough. If desired, sprinkle additional oregano, salt, and pepper, ending with your choice of cheeses. Recommended: grated Parmesan and provolone. Optional toppings: precooked sausage crumbles, pepperoni, sweet or hot pepper strips, anchovies, and mushrooms.

Bake at 400° for 25 to 30 minutes, or until crust is browned.

Note: The sauce can be used with precooked commercial pizza shells, or store-bought dough. Also, frozen bread dough can be allowed to thaw before stretching, rising, and adding the sauce.

♦ *Makes* about four pizzas

CSO Radiothon Pizza Party

by Evelyn Meine

*I*n 1976, The Chicago Symphony Orchestra held its first fund-raising radiothon. One of the premiums that was enthusiastically purchased for $100 was a pizza party for eight guests prepared by a management staff member—me. I promised a bevy of performing waitresses, also from the staff, to serve the party. This premium was offered two times, but was so in demand that I agreed to do seven more parties in the months to come.

The first party was held in a high-rise overlooking Lake Michigan. Armed with pizza fixings, Italian salad ingredients, and several gallons of jug wine, five ladies arrived to deliver the premium. Clad in red bandanna aprons and head kerchiefs and carrying several instruments, we gave the gathered music lovers an evening to remember.

In the following years, the parties were limited to two a year, mostly because the head cook (me) ran out of leisure time.

Evelyn's Stuffed Greens Pizza

FILLING

½ 8-ounce package cream cheese
   or 1 cup ricotta cheese

½ cup grated Romano cheese

2 egg yolks, divided

2 cloves garlic, chopped

Salt and pepper to taste

Red pepper flakes

Vegetable oil

Parsley

2 cups cooked rice

½ pound mustard greens, chopped

Cumin seeds

DOUGH

Double recipe of Grandma's pizza
   dough (page 49), divided, or
   2 pieces frozen bread/pizza
   dough

Use a 10-inch, greased springform pan. Put one piece of dough in pan and build up the sides. In a bowl, blend cheeses, 1 egg yolk, garlic, salt, pepper, red pepper flakes, oil, and parsley. Add rice and greens. Spread onto dough-lined pan. Roll out another loaf to cover. Pinch sides and seal. Mix remaining egg yolk and a little water; brush over top. Decorate top with cumin seeds. Allow crust to rise in warm place. Bake at 400 degrees for 40 to 50 minutes. Cool 10 minutes; serve.

BECK'S VARIATION

I use 1 cup ricotta cheese, 2 egg yolks, 1 cup Romano cheese, 3 to 4 cloves garlic, salt and pepper, vegetable oil, 1 cup cooked rice, a bunch of mustard greens, and thawed, drained frozen spinach and spread it all on two frozen pizza dough crusts. My theory is that you can use whatever proportions seem good to you. It tasted great!

◆ Makes one pizza

There are many variations of this. I didn't use rice when I made it, but Grandma did. You can also use four boxes frozen chopped spinach or Swiss chard (thawed and drained) instead of mustard greens. —Evelyn

Joe's Stuffed Manicotti

1 eggplant, cut into half-inch slices

1 onion, peeled and quartered

1 red pepper, seeded and quartered

3 small tomatoes, stem cut out

3 cloves elephant garlic, minced

Olive oil

1 egg

2 cups ricotta cheese

6 ounces shredded Asiago cheese

Salt and pepper

1 box uncooked manicotti
    (14 manicotti total)

Pinch of nutmeg

Traditional red sauce (see
    Grandma's Spaghetti Sauce
    [page 63] or use any other
    one you like)

Cook manicotti according to package directions, drain, and cool. Coat eggplant, onion, red pepper, tomatoes, and garlic with olive oil and roast at 350 degrees for 45 minutes. Remove from oven. Chop and strain tomatoes; add juice to red sauce. Chop up the roasted veggies and add egg, ricotta, half the Asiago, salt, pepper, and nutmeg. Mix with chopped tomato.

Stuff cooked manicotti with filling and place in a single layer in a 9×13-inch cake pan. Pour sauce over the stuffed manicotti and cover with remaining Asiago. Bake at 350 degrees for 30 minutes.

◆ Makes fourteen manicotti

Grandma's Spaghetti and Meatballs

Meatballs

1 pound ground chuck
1 clove garlic, minced
2 or 3 eggs
1/4 cup grated Romano cheese
1 1/2 to 2 cups bread crumbs
1 teaspoon salt

1 teaspoon pepper
1 handful chopped parsley
1 handful chopped celery leaves
1/2 cup water, more or less
3 tablespoons olive oil, plus
   some more

Grandma's Note: This recipe makes about eighteen meatballs. If you want to stretch the recipe, add more eggs and bread crumbs. If you like more tender meatballs, add more water.

Mix all ingredients well. Add a little water to get tender consistency that will hold together. Coat hands with oil and shape meat into balls. Heat oil in skillet. Add meatballs and turn often so they keep shape while they brown. Transfer to sauce pot, oil and all.

Sauce

1 28- to 30-ounce can whole or
   crushed tomatoes and 1 can
   water
1 28- to 30-ounce can tomato
   puree and 1 can water
   (Grandma removed the "and 1
   can water" in another recipe)

1 8-ounce can tomato paste and
   2 cans water
1 clove garlic, minced
1 teaspoon basil
2 teaspoons salt
1/2 teaspoon pepper
3 tablespoons sugar

Brown the garlic and add sauce ingredients. Stir and simmer until thick.

• *Serves* twelve, with enough to freeze after!

Note: These are Grandma's ingredients. No additional instructions given! But she does note that sauce can be made without meatballs for Spaghetti Marinara: Brown 2 cloves chopped garlic in 3 tablespoons oil, add ingredients, and simmer. Also, Anita notes that Grandma didn't always stick to the same number of cans and kinds of tomatoes. She adapted what she had on hand and somehow it always tasted good. Occasionally, she would even substitute other meats for meatballs: spare ribs, a pork chop, pork sausage, or braciole (see recipe on page 95).

Judy tastes Kate's attempt at Grandma's sauce.

When we were kids, Grandma often made a meatloaf instead of meatballs, cooking it in the sauce in the same way. She would slice leftover meatloaf for sandwiches—essentially bread between slices of bread if lots of crumbs were used in the meatloaf. —Anita

Sunday is a day that you don't want to spend a lot of time cooking. Just make your meatballs and sauce and have some pasta. —Grandma

The Spaghetti Winding Curse:
You must never wind your spaghetti on a fork while twirling the fork clockwise (while looking down from above) or you will surely get sauce on your white blouse/ shirt/socks/jockey shorts.
—Jody

SAUCE THOUGHTS FROM GRANDMA

I always put sugar in because I don't like the taste of raw tomato. But not everybody adds it. I think it makes all kinds of a difference. A little tomato goes a long way.

If you make too much sauce, you can freeze it and use it another time. Label it with how many meatballs are in there and what day you froze it.

The sauce has to be thick. If you start it early in the morning on Sunday, by noon it should be done. But if you don't have a man, you can make your own hours and eat it any time. You can make it on Saturday and all you have to do is heat it up the next day if that's when you want it.

Most important thing: The meatballs have to cook in the sauce. They are what flavors it.

Evelyn's Pasta Sauce

⅓ cup vegetable oil or meatball
    drippings (add oil if drippings
    don't amount to ⅓ cup)
3 large cloves garlic, chopped or
    crushed (more if desired)
1 28- to 30-ounce can crushed
    tomatoes
1 28- to 30-ounce can tomato
    puree
1 6-ounce can tomato paste

1½ cans of water (28- to
    30-ounce can)
⅛ teaspoon sugar
1+ teaspoon each dried basil and
    Italian seasoning
1 teaspoon salt
½ teaspoon black pepper
1 small onion, chopped
1 cup Burgundy wine (optional)
Grandma's Meatballs, page 63

Heat oil or meatball drippings over medium heat in large saucepan. Add garlic and brown lightly. Add tomatoes, tomato puree, and tomato paste (which must be diluted before adding for better mixing—see note). Add water and all other ingredients and bring to boil. Adjust spices to your taste. Add meatballs and cover. Reduce heat and simmer, stirring frequently. Cook for at least an hour, or until thick.

Note: When opening tomato paste, it's best to open both ends of the can and slide the paste into a bowl. Add about the same amount of water as the can, and whisk together. Then add to sauce.

VARIATION

For a slightly different flavor, add your favorite beef, veal, or pork cuts —brown and add to sauce.

• Makes enough for 2 pounds of spaghetti, about 8–10 servings. There may be leftover sauce.

Grandma's Pasta Fazool

(A.K.A. PASTA E FAGIOLE)

Depending on whether Grandma had celery on hand, this was a quick-fix kind of dish and it would be made and enjoyed with or without celery.   —Anita

¾ pound ditalini

¼ cup vegetable oil

2 or 3 cloves garlic, chopped

1 8-ounce can tomato sauce

1 15-ounce can crushed tomatoes

Basil, salt, and pepper to taste

About a handful tender inner tips of celery leaves, chopped (optional)

1 tablespoon sugar, if tomatoes are too acidy

1 18-ounce can great northern or cannellini beans, undrained

Chopped parsley for garnish

Grated Parmesan or Romano cheese to taste

While ditalini cooks, prepare sauce as follows. Heat oil. Add garlic and brown lightly. Stir in tomato sauce and crushed tomatoes. Add basil, salt, pepper, and celery leaves. Add sugar if tomatoes are too acidic. Add great northern or cannellini beans, undrained.

Simmer sauce until ditalini is done. Drain water from the ditalini, reserving some. Return ditalini to cooking pot. Add sauce and bean mixture and mix well. If too dry, add some of the reserved water. Pour into serving dish and top with chopped parsley. Serve with grated cheese.

• *Makes* six servings

This was Grandma's favorite dish. She liked it soupy, so she always added enough cooking water to make it that way. Her cupboard always had shallow soup bowls that were seldom used for anything but pasta fazool. I never saw Grandma use onion in pasta fazool, but I made it once with ½ cup chopped onion, and she liked it a lot.   —Anita

Mine is pretty much the same. Sometimes I like to add carrots or chick peas or diced white potatoes.

When Evelyn added other ingredients, Grandma threw a tantrum. Evelyn called it creative; Grandma called it ruining the pasta fazool. —*Judy*

PAVAROTTI AND PASTA FAZOOL

by Evelyn Meine

In April 1991, under the direction of Maestro Georg Solti, the Chicago Symphony Orchestra presented a concert version of *Otello* with Luciano Pavarotti, Kiri Te Kanawa, and other notable performers. I offered to present one of my legendary pizza parties as an after-concert treat for the Soltis and their guests, which included the guest artists and others involved in the *Otello* production. The party would be held in the Solti hotel suite.

My daughter-in-law Sue arrived early in the evening to help prepare the food. An intimate group of about twenty guests gathered, but Pavarotti was a no-show. Mrs. Solti eventually phoned the Pavarotti suite in the same hotel, only to find he was not feeling well, and apologies were offered. Mrs. Solti immediately suggested that food be prepared for the great tenor and his entourage and that it could be delivered to them.

Checking the food supply, the kitchen crew found cans of tomatoes, pasta, olive oil, beans, and various spices. Using a solitary pot, pasta e fagioli was improvised. With Valerie Solti heading the rescue squad, a choice bottle of wine in

hand, a pizza carrier and a pasta pot carrier were welcomed into the sitting room of the noted singer. Pavarotti was semi-reclined on a lounge, using an enormous absorbent fabric to mop his brow, and he welcomed the group in weak whispers. Mrs. Solti went to him with comforting words, presented him with the gifts, and after a few minutes took leave to return to her guests.

The story isn't over.

The following evening, after a repeat performance of *Otello*, I went backstage to pay my respects to Maestro Solti and to Pavarotti. Before I reached Pavarotti's dressing room, Valerie Solti pulled me aside and whispered, "Luciano wondered if there was any more of the pasta e fagioli." Unfortunately, the pasta brigade of the night before didn't perform an encore.

Alexis's Pasta Fazool

Try this variation if you like more veggies and a little more kick.

Olive or vegetable oil
½ clove garlic, chopped (optional)
1 small onion, chopped fine
Celery leaves and small hearts,
    chopped, about ¼ cup or less
    (optional)
1 to 3 tablespoons dried basil
1 to 2 teaspoons dried oregano
Salt and pepper to taste
A couple shakes of red pepper
    flakes
1 15-ounce can stewed tomatoes
    (add any leftover canned
    tomatoes you may have or sauce
    [small amount] or overripe
    tomatoes, chopped)

⅔ 15- or 16-ounce box of the
    SMALLEST ditalini you can
    find (or little tiny shells—
    sometimes you can't find
    ditalini)
1 to 3 tablespoons sugar
1 15-ounce can cannellini beans,
    undrained
1 15-ounce can vegetarian baked
    beans
1 8-ounce can corn

1. Cover bottom of heavy sauce pan with oil and heat. Brown garlic slightly, then add onion and celery leaves and cook until translucent, while adding basil, oregano, salt, pepper, and red pepper flakes. Heat through without browning the onions.

2. Add tomatoes. Heat through.

3. Boil water and add pasta. Cook until well done, not al dente.

4. While pasta is cooking, add sugar to sauce to taste—just get the bitterness out of the tomatoes.

5. Heat through for about 10 to 15 minutes.

6. When pasta is done, don't drain all water out . . . leave water level just below the top of the pasta. Pour pasta into sauce and stir. Then add beans and corn. Heat through.

7. Serve immediately, or later, or leave in fridge overnight—whatever.

8. SPRINKLE LOTS OF EXPENSIVE PARMESAN/ROMANO/ PECORINO or any other stinky cheese on top.

9. Eat lots and lots of bowlsful . . . eat it cold later. Have for breakfast the next morning.

♦ *Serves* six to twelve, depending on how hungry you are!

Evelyn's Pasta with Clam Sauce

6 tablespoons olive oil

1 teaspoon chopped garlic

1 cup clam broth

¼ cup dry white wine

1 8-ounce can clams

1 pound spaghettini

2 tablespoons soft butter

Chopped parsley for garnish

Parmesan cheese

Fresh clams can also be used.   —Evelyn

Heat olive oil in skillet. Cook garlic in oil until brown (30 seconds). Pour in clam broth and dry white wine. Cook until foam disappears and sauce equals ½ cup. Just before serving, add clams and cook several minutes.

In the meantime, cook spaghettini. Drain. Toss with butter. Add sauce, and sprinkle with parsley. Serve with Parmesan cheese.

VARIATION

Recently I added diced pepperoni and it was great!

◆ Serves **four**

Grandma's Pasta Alberto

Grandma actually called this "the pasta with the vegetables." I call it "Pasta Alberto," because that's the restaurant where we first tasted it. Grandma later simplified it by cooking frozen mixed vegetables according to package directions, sauteing onion with garlic, combining them, and adding chopped olives.   —Anita

1 pound vermicelli
3 carrots, chopped fine
3 celery stalks, chopped fine
½ bunch parsley, chopped fine

1 medium onion, chopped fine
½ cup olive oil
1 12-ounce can tuna
1 4¼-ounce can chopped black
    olives (or chopped ripe ones
    from larger can)
1 4-ounce can chopped mushrooms
1 2-ounce can anchovies
4 cloves garlic, coarsely minced
½ cup water
Salt and pepper to taste
Parmesan or Romano cheese

Grandma teaches Janice (left) and Judy to make Pasta Alberto on one summer visit in the mid-'90s.

1. Pasta: Cook vermicelli according to package directions. Meanwhile, prepare topping and sauce.

2. Topping: Sauté carrots, celery, parsley, and onion in olive oil until tender. Drain tuna, black olives, mushrooms, and anchovies and mix in with vegetables. When all ingredients are heated, remove from oil with slotted spoon and set aside. Reserve oil for sauce.

3. Sauce: If necessary, add enough olive oil to reserved oil to replace original amount. Sauté garlic until slightly browned. Add water and salt and pepper to taste.

4. Presentation: Drain vermicelli and return to cooking pot. Mix in the garlic sauce.

5. Transfer to serving platter and add topping. Serve with freshly grated Parmesan or Romano cheese.

◆ *Serves* six

HOMEMADE PASTA, GRANDMA STYLE

by Roxanne Aubrey

I am the lucky inheritor of Grandma's pasta machine from the late 1920s. I remember her always complaining about it: "Oh, it's old and it rolls the pasta crooked. You don't want that."

I finally got my hands on the mythical rolling pasta machine. And yup, it rolled them crooked alright. I, however, have something that Grandma didn't have: Tommy! One afternoon with my boyfriend, and that machine was rolling perfect pasta! I'm sure Grandpa could have fixed it, but I bet she preferred to complain about the machine rather than have it fixed. One less thing she had to make from scratch.

For every person eating pasta, you need:

1 cup flour	⅛ teaspoon salt
1 egg	Water as needed
1 teaspoon olive oil	

First, mix everything together and beat the crap out of the dough in a food processor (using the plastic blade). Then,

taste it to make sure it's good—not too salty or bland. Let it rest for 5 to 10 minutes, divide it up into small, golf ball-sized balls, and flatten them out with your hands. Flour them extensively and then start to crank. The machine has a bunch of different settings, so start on the thickest. I roll them all at one setting, go down a few sizes, reflour them and run them through the machine again, repeating until they're the size I want. Make sure they're not too ridiculously long, though. I mean, think about it.

Then let the noodles dry for a bit. This is a pain in my shoebox-size apartment, because the only place flat enough for me to dry them on is my bed. So I lay out the terry cloth bath towels on the bed and let the noodles dry for 10 to 20 minutes.

Then you cut them. This machine has a spaghetti, a linguine, and a vermicelli cutter. When they come out the other side, some will be too short to use. These, of course, must be eaten right away. I like to lay the cut ones on a cookie sheet with some corn flour or semolina flour. Not necessary, but it helps the noodles not stick together or to the cookie sheet. So the process is this:

1. Retrieve a flat noodle from the bedroom.
2. Cut.
3. Munch.
4. Lay over corn flour.
5. Munch a little more.
6. Walk to the bedroom and grab another.
7. Cut.
8. Munch.

And so on.

Cook the noodles in lots of boiling, salted water. The coolest thing about fresh pasta is that it literally takes about 3 to 4 minutes to cook. The uncool-

est thing is that by the time you're ready to eat, you're so filled with all the little raw bits of pasta, you can't really enjoy the meal.

I remember Grandma rolling out pasta dough for raviolis. The rolling and rolling. Man, it was a lot of work. Yet she still managed to make them prettier than mine ever looked (sigh). This process is not that different. And, if I had a kitchen that was bigger than the bathroom on a Greyhound bus, it would actually be enjoyable. I've used the electric machines, and they don't make awful pasta, but the process just isn't tactile enough. It's just not as satisfying. An old, hand-cranked machine is definitely the way to go. Look on eBay. There are lots of them there.

Grandma's Oily-Oilies

(A.K.A., AGLIO E OLIO, OR WHITE MACARONI)

½ cup olive oil

4 cloves garlic, chopped

Salt to taste

½ teaspoon pepper

1 2-ounce can flat anchovies,
   drained (optional)

½ cup water from cooked pasta

1 pound capellini or vermicelli,
   cooked

Heat oil. Add garlic and lightly brown. Add salt and pepper. Lower heat and add anchovies. Cook until they break up fine. Pour sauce over cooked pasta and add a little cooking water. Serve with cheese.

♦ *Serves* six to eight or even more since it's one of many dishes served at Christmas.

Note from Judy: You don't need as much pasta if you're using capellini—a little goes a long way. Same with vermicelli. You don't need as much as you do with regular spaghetti.

EVELYN'S VARIATION

Add a handful of pepperoni instead of anchovies.

JOE'S VARIATION

For when you want the oily-oily taste without the garlic breath (possibly when you're on a date): Cook pasta and sauté 1 2-ounce can of anchovies (drained) in 1 tablespoon olive oil; add lots of fresh or dried rosemary and stir sauce into pasta; add ¼ cup chopped walnuts and garnish with a pinch of cayenne pepper.

Kate's Vodka Pasta

This recipe is actually stolen from friend and professional chef Doug Sohn, who taught me how to make it. I have the feeling I probably don't remember the finer points. But the great thing about it is that it's pretty hard to screw up . . . I've made a lot of different variations of it, and it's always good! (Thanks, Doug.)   —Kate

Olive oil, enough to cover bottom
of large skillet
½ to 1 teaspoon crushed red
pepper flakes
3 to 4 cloves garlic, crushed
½ pound to 1 pound shrimp,
shelled and deveined
1 to 2 15-ounce cans diced
tomatoes

1 16-ounce box penne, bow ties,
or mostaccioli
Salt and pepper to taste
Vodka, about ⅓ cup
2 to 5 teaspoons heavy whipping
cream, depending on how
creamy you want it
1 to 3 teaspoons chopped fresh
basil for garnish

In a large skillet, heat oil. Add red pepper flakes and garlic. Add shrimp, allow to cook 2 to 3 minutes. Add tomatoes and juice, and simmer. Meanwhile, add pasta to boiling water.

Taste sauce and add salt and pepper, if desired. As sauce is simmering, hold thumb lightly over top of vodka bottle and pour vodka into sauce, making two circles over skillet. Let vodka cook off for a few minutes and add a teaspoon or two of heavy whipping cream. When the pasta is done, drain and add to skillet and spoon everything all over each other. Serve on heated plates with fresh basil on top.

• Serves four to six

Main Courses

Grandma's Rosemary Chicken

This recipe is an old classic and is traditionally part of celebrations, holidays, and other large meals.

Olive oil to coat pan
4 to 6 chicken pieces
1 or 2 cloves garlic, chopped
Salt and pepper to taste

Crushed dried rosemary to taste
Chopped parsley to taste
White wine for basting (optional)

Preheat oven to 425 degrees. Oil bottom of roasting pan. Arrange chicken in pan. Add garlic, then enough salt, pepper, rosemary, and parsley to cover the pieces. Mix with hands until chicken is coated with ingredients. Bake at 425 degrees for 15 minutes and lower to 350 degrees for another 45 minutes or until done. Stir occasionally.

◆ *Serves* four to six

Optional: Add white or sweet potatoes, or both.

Grandma would use white wine on special occasions.
    —Anita

EVELYN'S VARIATION

Combine marinade ingredients and marinate chicken 2 or 3 hours before cooking. Can also add ⅓ cup white vinegar or lemon juice to ingredients.

◆

The following menu is an example of a traditional Easter meal, according to Grandma:

Wedding Soup   29
Spaghetti and Meatballs   63
Rosemary Chicken   83
Stuffed Artichokes   113
Lamb Cake   217

◆ ◆ ◆

Anita's Sour Cream Chicken

6 boneless, skinless chicken pieces

8 ounces sour cream

2 to 4 cups seasoned small-crumb stuffing

½ cup melted butter or margarine

1. Wipe off chicken, removing any moisture, and coat with sour cream.

2. Roll in seasoned stuffing.

3. Arrange in ovenproof casserole.

4. Drizzle with melted butter or margarine.

5. Cover with aluminum foil.

6. Bake at 350 degrees for 1 hour, then uncover and bake for another 20 minutes.

♦ *Serves* six

Note about amounts: I'm giving you these measurements, but I don't really believe in them. The thing is, you make enough chicken as you need, and then all else follows. Amounts are unpredictable because the size of the pieces is unknown. Also, the viscosity of the sour cream has a lot to do with how many crumbs will adhere, and even whether or not the sour cream will stick to the chicken. That makes a lot of difference in the amounts!

Beck's Basic Chicken for Two

Olive oil (enough to coat chicken
on both sides)
Two chicken breasts
4 cloves garlic, minced
Juice of one lemon

Handful of fresh basil, chopped
¼ cup to ½ cup grated Parmesan
cheese

Preheat oven to 350 degrees. Put small amount of oil in baking pan. Put
chicken in pan and roll it around in the oil to coat. Add generous amount
of minced garlic. Squeeze a small amount of lemon juice onto the chicken.
Place fresh basil on chicken, mostly covering the surface. Cover with grated
Parmesan cheese. Bake for 30 minutes, or until done. Don't overcook, lest
the chicken become too dry.

♦ *Serves* two

THE SEARCH FOR THE KILLER GARLIC

by *Anita DeVivo*

Mom maintains that garlic flavors have weakened over the years and you just can't get good garlic anymore. She and I have sampled garlic from every grocery store and produce stand in New Castle. Janice has sent strings from Dean and Deluca and from Balducci's in New York. And Alexis has consulted with her garlic guru in Connecticut. Nothing turned up until last summer, when Jody bought a bunch at Michelangelo's flea market outside of New Castle. Grandma cooked with half of the bunch and then declared, "These are the garlics to plant."

And so, last October I did. I followed Pop's rules for planting garlic:

1. Plant cloves 1 foot apart.

2. No more than 2 inches deep.

3. Wide end down.

4. Pointy end up.

5. Have a glass of wine.

Text reprinted from *The Mama DeVivo Newsletter*, Issue 15, September 15, 1995

The garlic began to throw shoots in February, because the winter was mild. Eventually they formed these little bulbs on top that looked pretty interesting.

They must have thrown seeds out, because I found a garlic plant around the corner with the tomatoes.

Now the tradition is that you don't pick garlic until St. Margaret's Day, July 20. People who don't know that wait for the leaves to wilt and then dig, whether it's June or August. I think if the leaves hadn't wilted by July 20, I wouldn't have started digging.

A week before I planned to dig, I heard that you're supposed to cut those white bulbs off if you want big garlic. Where was that piece of wisdom when I needed it? Resigned to getting tiny garlic, I dug. Here are the results.

After Grandma did the acid test and sniffed them out, she declared that they passed!

Mom's old neighbor Arthur Budelazze used to hose his garlic down and leave it in the sun, so that's what I did. (I couldn't remember what Pop did.) Then I cut off the top bulbs. I couldn't resist opening one of them. It was full of clovelets, which I understand are plantable, but I'm not sure what you get. From the looks of the little blossoms in the cluster, this is where the allium flower develops. I put one of the bulbs in a glass of water to see whether it would bloom, but it didn't.

Next year I'll let one go to flower to see what happens. Pop had grown an allium back in 1983. It was dramatic—3 feet tall, the size and shape of a cantaloupe, perfectly round, with a light violet color. I kept it dry in my office for months, until one of my coworkers asked for it. You can get them at flower stands in big cities for close to $10.

Now, here's the question: What will I plant for next year? When I thought I was going to get inferior garlic because I hadn't cut those bulbs off, I nosed around for some more local killer garlic. I went to Michelangelo's again, to

Roger's flea market in Ohio, I got some garlic from Will's mother, Nancy, who is a master gardener, and some of Mom's favorite brand at the grocery store.

I laid them all out to compare the size. Roger's was by far the largest, mine the second largest, the grocery's third, Michelangelo's fourth, and Nancy's the smallest (she admits she's not so good at garlic).

When I asked Mom to tell me which she liked best, she liked Michelangelo's again, but mine was a close second (only because they weren't as clean and white, I suspect). I'm sorry now that I didn't buy more.

I went back Sunday to get some more. I remembered that the farmer had several front teeth missing, but either he wasn't there, or he got his teeth fixed and I didn't recognize him. Too bad. The seed had come from Italy via an Italian steelworker in Youngstown, and somehow that made it more choice. We'll have to make do with my garlic and what's left of Michelangelo's.

My lessons out of this year's crop are these:

1. Get the farmer's name and number.

2. Cut those tops off.

3. According to Nancy, feed the garlic (did she feed hers?).

4. The straight-stemmed garlic seems to be more powerful than the soft-stemmed kind that can be braided.

I guess it's time to stop the benign neglect. Next time I'm in a garden store I'll look around for the plant food. I'll feed once after planting, then again early next spring. But maybe I'll leave some of the next crop unfed. After all, did all those Italian farmers buy boxes of blue and pink stuff to put into the ground?

Evelyn's Chicken Cacciatore

⅓ cup oil (olive preferred)

3 pounds chicken pieces, about 8 pieces

2 slices bacon, diced

2 medium onions, sliced

1 4½-ounce can mushrooms, drained

1 to 2 tablespoons chopped parsley

1 teaspoon dried basil

1 clove garlic, chopped

⅛ teaspoon salt

⅛ teaspoon pepper

1 cup dry white wine

1 28- to 30-ounce can crushed tomatoes

Heat oil in Dutch oven. Brown chicken pieces in oil; remove pieces to platter. Add bacon to pan, cook 1 minute. Add onions and mushrooms. Brown vegetables and then return chicken to pot. Add parsley, basil, garlic, salt, pepper, wine, and tomatoes. Cook covered in Dutch oven at 375 degrees for 15 minutes; reduce heat to 350 degrees and cook for another 15 minutes.

◆ *Serves* six to eight

This may be cooked in a pressure cooker at 10 pounds of pressure for approximately 25 minutes. Refer to your cooker's instruction book. —Evelyn

Joe's Stir-Fried Chicken with Pineapple

This is a remarkably easy stir-fry that tastes great and makes a great meal when served with rice. The fresh ginger gives it a bite, though!   —Joe

1 ¼ pounds boneless, skinless chicken breasts, thinly sliced at an angle

2 tablespoons cornstarch

4 tablespoons sunflower oil (peanut oil works, too)

1 small onion, thinly sliced

1 garlic clove, crushed

2 inches fresh ginger root, peeled and cut into matchsticks

1 fresh pineapple, peeled, cored, and cubed, or 1 15-ounce can of pineapple chunks in natural juice

2 tablespoons dark soy sauce

6 to 8 green onions, white bulbs left whole, green tops sliced

Salt and pepper to taste

1. Heat oil in wok or frying pan. Toss strips of chicken into the cornstarch. Stir-fry in hot oil until tender.

2. Remove chicken from wok or frying pan and keep warm. Reheat the oil and stir-fry the onion, garlic, and ginger until soft, but not brown. Add pineapple with the juice (if canned) or ½ cup of water, if using fresh pineapple.

3. Stir in the soy sauce and return the chicken to wok.

4. Season to taste. Add the green onion bulbs and half of the sliced green tops. Stir well, then transfer to serving platter. Garnish with remaining green onion tops.

◆ It's important to use the right oil when stir-frying. Corn oil burns at a much lower temperature than either peanut or sunflower oil. Olive oil is somewhere in between. I've had reasonable luck substituting olive oil, but corn oil just doesn't work.

◆ It's more important to do all your prep work before starting to stir-fry. Once you start cooking, you won't have time to cut, slice, dice, etc.

◆ *Serves* four to six

Evelyn's Beef Burgundy

4 to 5 pounds lean beef chunks

Red wine (enough to cover beef chunks)

$\frac{1}{3}$ cup bacon drippings

Oil (vegetable and/or olive), about $\frac{1}{4}$ inch in bottom of pan

A little butter

4 tablespoons flour

1 package onion soup mix

3 to 4 cloves garlic, minced

$\frac{1}{4}$ teaspoon dried thyme

Small handful of parsley, chopped

1 medium onion, chopped

3 carrots, chopped

1 pound mushrooms

$\frac{3}{4}$ cup celery leaves

1 or 2 bay leaves

1. Place beef chunks in large bowl, cover with wine, place in refrigerator, and marinate overnight. Drain marinated beef on paper towels, reserving marinade. Brown in bacon drippings, oil, and a little butter. When browned, remove meat and place in ovenproof casserole.

2. Add flour to drippings and bring to a boil to make a thin gravy. Add wine from marinade and enough additional liquid (3 parts wine to 1 part water) to make about 3 to 4 cups.

3. Add soup mix, garlic, thyme, and parsley.

4. Cook together until all is blended and slightly thick, then pour over meat; cover.

5. Simmer in 300-degree oven for 2 hours.

6. Meanwhile, parboil onions, carrots, mushrooms, celery, and bay leaf and add to casserole in oven after 1$\frac{1}{2}$ hours of cooking time and cook the remaining half hour.

• *Serves* eight to ten

For those who are Gen Xers or even Gen Yers, to "parboil" means to plunge into boiling water and cook for a short period of time. I asked Aunt Ev. —Kate

On bay leaves: I once almost choked on a bay leaf, so now I always put it in either a tea strainer or a cheese cloth—or, if the leaf doesn't break, I put a toothpick through the middle. —Evelyn

Beck's Emergency Meatloaf

I actually adapted this from my mom's meatloaf recipe when I was in a pinch to come up with something. It was my turn to cook for my housemates in graduate school, and this was the first thing I made. I knew it was a hit, because when I cooked it, their eyes grew wide with the realization that I could cook. My well-kept secret was out. It goes great with fresh green beans and Anita's Sweet Potatoes Rosemary (page 148 in the "Side Dishes" chapter).

1 7-ounce jar roasted red peppers, drained and chopped

½ cup mayonnaise

1 tablespoon Worcestershire sauce

2 teaspoons chopped garlic (jarred garlic is fine)

1 teaspoon hot pepper sauce

1 teaspoon salt

2 pounds ground beef

1 cup bread crumbs (I prefer just ripping up white bread from the loaf)

Preheat oven to 350 degrees. In a large bowl, whisk roasted peppers, mayonnaise, Worcestershire sauce, garlic, hot pepper sauce, and salt. Crumble ground beef into the bowl. Add the bread crumbs and mix thoroughly. You can be liberal with the red peppers and/or bread crumbs until you get the desired mushy mass of meat. (I may have also added Parmesan cheese, by the way. I can't remember!) Transfer the mixture to a 9 × 5 × 13-inch loaf pan, mounding slightly.

At this point, you can add ketchup, barbecue sauce, or chili sauce over the top. I don't find it necessary.

Bake for about 1 hour 20 minutes, periodically pouring out the juices (not too often though!). Let the loaf rest on a rack for 10 minutes before serving.

♦ *Serves* four to six

Evelyn's Braciole

This is a versatile dish adapted from what my mother used to make. You can add it to any sauce, which will give it a whole new taste, or keep it on the side. If you add it to the sauce, it will become so tender it will practically fall apart. It can also work as a very decorative dish, served on the side of any pasta, potatoes, or rice. The meat should be about ¼-inch thick, but if it doesn't come that way from the store, don't fret—you can pound it with a mallet to tenderize it and get it as thin as you want. Grandma never really made this for any special occasion, but if she found the right cut of meat or if we hadn't had it in a while, she would make it instead of meatballs for pasta.   —Evelyn

¼-inch-thick round steak,
   1 to 1½ pounds
Olive oil or margarine, enough to
   coat meat
2 cloves garlic, chopped
¼ cup each grated Parmesan and
   Romano cheese
½ cup each chopped celery leaves
   and parsley leaves

1 egg
½ cup bread crumbs
Salt and pepper to taste
⅓ cup raisins (optional)
1 egg, beaten with
   1 tablespoon water
Flour, enough to coat for dredging
Grandma's Spaghetti Sauce
   (page 63) (optional)

Using one slice of thin round steak, prepare as follows: Pound with meat mallet. Rub oil or margarine over the surface of the meat. Mix together garlic, cheese, celery and parsley leaves, egg, bread crumbs, salt, pepper, and raisins; spoon over surface of meat. Roll steak jelly roll fashion and tie or skewer securely. Carefully dip rolled steak into beaten egg and water, then flour. Sauté on all sides just until golden brown. Add to spaghetti sauce whole and cook for 1 hour 30 minutes, if desired. Remove from sauce. Allow to rest so that it can hold its shape when string or skewers are removed. Using a very sharp knife, carefully slice into ½-inch rounds and arrange on serving platter. Provide additional spaghetti sauce for those who want to dress it, if desired. *To cook separately, add about ½-inch beef broth or water to bottom of baking dish, cover, and cook in 300-degree oven until liquid is absorbed and meat is fork-tender.

◆ *Serves* four or five

Judy's Ground Beef Stroganoff

This recipe is based on one that I found in a cookbook that was given to me as a wedding present.   —Judy

½ cup minced onion

1 clove garlic, minced

¼ cup butter

1 pound ground beef, crumbled

2 tablespoons flour

2 teaspoons salt

Pepper to taste

½ pound fresh mushrooms, sliced, or 1 8-ounce can, drained

1 can cream of mushroom soup

1 cup sour cream

Chopped parsley for garnish

1 16-ounce bag egg noodles, cooked

Sauté onion and garlic in butter. Stir in meat and brown. Stir in flour, salt, pepper, and mushrooms. Cook 5 minutes. Stir in soup. Cook 5 minutes. Stir in sour cream. Heat through. Do not let it come to a boil. Garnish with parsley and serve over hot noodles.

◆ *Serves* eight

G.G.'s Swiss Steak

1 to 1½ pounds round steak,
   enough for four people
Salt and pepper to taste
Flour for dredging
1 to 2 onions, chopped

4 potatoes, peeled and sliced
1 16-ounce can sliced carrots,
   or 2 large fresh carrots, pared
   and sliced
1 16-ounce can chopped tomatoes,
   undrained

Cover steak with salt, pepper, and flour, then pound with edge of plate or table knife.

Brown steak on both sides on stovetop. Then, remove and place in oven-proof dish and cover with layer of onions, potatoes, carrots, and tomatoes. Add additional salt and pepper to taste. Add water if necessary. Cook at 350 degrees until tender, about 1½ hours.

♦ *Serves* **four**

G.G. always cooked this in an iron skillet, and that's the way I do it. Believe me, it works better and tastes better that way! —Babs

Note: Amounts of potatoes, carrots, and onions can vary according to taste and preference.

Grandma DeMasi's Peppers and Tomatoes al Gennaro

"Gennaro" is my Grandfather DeMasi's name. This is something that Grandma DeMasi used to make—and it's really good!   —Evelyn

2 tablespoons olive oil

2 garlic cloves, chopped very fine

3½ cups fresh tomatoes, cored, blanched, peeled, and chopped coarse (or canned plum tomatoes, drained)

1 teaspoon salt

1 tablespoon chopped, fresh basil (or 1 teaspoon dried)

½ teaspoon sugar

⅓ cup olive oil

1 large Italian sausage (¼ pound), cut on a slant into 1-inch slices

2 pounds green peppers, seeded and quartered

2 onions, sliced (about 1 cup)

Pepper, ground fresh, to taste

⅓ cup dry red wine or Madeira (optional)

1. Heat 2 tablespoons olive oil in a large skillet; add garlic and sauté until lightly browned. Add tomatoes, salt, basil, and sugar. Cook over medium heat for 30 minutes.

2. While tomatoes are cooking, heat the remaining ⅓ cup olive oil in another skillet, and brown the sausage slices well on all sides. Transfer the slices with a slotted spoon to the tomato mixture in the other skillet.

3. Reserve the oil in which the sausage cooked in the skillet. Add peppers to same skillet and toss them well. Sauté for about 8 to 10 minutes, then add the onions, and cook for another 20 minutes, or until vegetables are softened and slightly charred. Add them to the tomato mixture, and cook together for an additional 5 to 10 minutes. Adjust seasonings to taste. Add wine or Madeira (if you wish) to the skillet after the peppers and onions have cooked. Deglaze the pan, and add the liquid to the tomato and pepper mixture before the last 5 or 10 minutes of cooking.

◆ *Serves* four to six

GRANDPA'S GARDEN

This is an excerpt from a conversation I had with Grandma when I spent a week cooking with her and Anita. —Kate

We had a garden. That's how we learned many things. My mother had one before my husband. We grew up with it. In those days, during the Depression, all the boys used to go down in the garden. We lived in a house where there was lots of room for planting. In Mahoningtown, I suppose you found the best boys who knew how to make a garden.

Joe knew how to garden from the Old Country. He was nine when he came here, and he knew everything. In the old country, they were more educated about where you could make a garden and where you couldn't . . . it was more common over there than it was here.

But when the boys came from Italy they knew how to do it. I went to school with Joe, but I didn't really know him. He was just a boy with big black hair. I didn't know him until later when we were both singing in the church choir, when I was about fifteen or sixteen. He was working already for the railroad. I thought he was cute. We would sing in the choir,

and he had a good voice—he was a musician. When we left church, we sang along the way home.

My mother didn't know until late that I had a boyfriend, and she didn't like it. "You do everything behind my back!" she said. She'd found out from my aunt before I told her. One night Joe came over and said to my mom, "I'm here because I want your approval that I can go out with Helen."

I was flabbergasted. I didn't think he had the nerve. But he was Italian. He had guts. All she said to him was, "Now you ask me, after everybody knows about it!" Later that night, my dad said to my mom, "Listen. I've known about the two of them for a long time. He's not a bad guy." I think my mother got over it soon. She just put up a front and pretended that she was mad.

Joe was a real good guy. He was very well brought up . . . he had big sisters, and he did things pretty right. He was a pretty good boy, and he didn't cause trouble. We decided to get married when I was eighteen. He was the best guy in the world.

And he had a garden. Corn, cabbage, peppers, zucchini, tomatoes, green beans—all the vegetables you buy at the market. And garlic, basil, oregano, and other herbs.

Grandma's Stuffed Peppers

6 medium green peppers

4 cups bread crumbs

2 cloves garlic, minced

2 tablespoons olive oil

2 tablespoons minced parsley

¼ cup Romano cheese

1 or 2 tomatoes, blanched, peeled,
and crushed

1 cup corn (optional)

Handful of raisins (optional)

2 lightly beaten eggs (optional)
(Note: one of Grandma's
recipes says "3 eggs")

Salt and pepper to taste

2 cups tomato sauce (leftover pasta
sauce is good)

1 tablespoon olive oil

Set oven to 350 degrees. Wash peppers, cut in half lengthwise, remove seeds. Mix other ingredients (except tomato sauce and 1 tablespoon vegetable oil). Use the 1 tablespoon of oil to coat the peppers with hands inside and out. Stuff the peppers with mixture. Arrange in a shallow baking dish with the green side up. Cook for 15 or 20 minutes. Then carefully turn peppers over and cover with sauce. Baste with sauce every so often until peppers are done (about 45 minutes).

Note: peppers may also be stuffed whole. If stuffed whole, cook on their sides first, then with stuffing end up, so stuffing is covered with sauce.

♦ Serves **twelve**

Three generations making Grandma's Stuffed Peppers

JODY'S LESSONS ON GRILLING TO HIS DAUGHTER

Kate: Daddy?

    Jody: Yes, my little cupcake?

    K: Tell me how to grill!

J: Never grill without a martini.

K: But how do you make a hamburger?

J: Make sure the hamburger patties are equa-thick out to the edges. Nothing screws up a hamburger like thin rims that burn before the interior parts are even warmed up. And these days, no hamburger should be cooked too rare.

K: How about steaks?

J: The trick to cooking steaks is to have them all, the rares, the mediums, the wells, and the half-steps in between, finish at exactly the same time. Which means you have to put them on the fire at different times. This takes practice. Also, when you salt and pepper and maybe garlic the steaks before you put them on the fire, take a wooden spoon and beat the hell out of the steaks so the seasonings stick and don't fall off.

K: What else can you tell me?

J: At McDonald's, they tell their cooks not to salt meat before it's cooked because it will make it less tender, but I can't tell the difference. Also, the quality of meat you cook is really important. If you know where you can get restaurant-quality meats, go for it. And finally, don't forget, never grill without a martini.

K: How about kebabs?

J: Those are a mystery to me. Mine never end up tender. And the veggies keep falling off. And when I turn the skewers, the meat doesn't turn, it stays on the same side.

K: Hot dogs?

J: The biggest mistake most people make regarding hot dogs is they think of the wiener as the most important ingredient. Just the opposite is true. It's the least important ingredient. Not only do all wieners taste basically the same, what they taste like doesn't really matter. It's the taste of the stuff you put on them that's really important. Think of the wiener as a carrier. And the bun as a holder (which means you must insist on using buns that don't break into two parts when you open them). Of course, what you put on your hot dogs is a matter of individual taste, and there will always be a division between the mustard people and the ketchup people. But I can't help but believe that if everybody had the chance to grow up in New Castle and eat Coney Island hot dogs with burn-your-mouth and sweat-your-hair chili on them, they'd never have them any other way. Judy has a recipe for it that comes very close to that chili. In fact, I think Judy's recipe, which she got from Ralphy, tastes more like the way Coney Island's chili used to taste than what you'll find in New Castle now. I think they've taken some of the burn out.

Ralphy's Coney Island Chili

1 ½ pounds ground beef

2 tablespoons vegetable oil

2 tablespoons chopped onion

2 tablespoons salt

2 tablespoons cayenne pepper

4 tablespoons chili powder

1 tablespoon dried sage

1 tablespoon paprika

1 tablespoon black pepper

1 8-ounce can tomato paste

2 quarts water

Brown meat and onion in oil until onion is limp. Add other ingredients. Cook down for about 2 hours.

♦ *Makes* enough for a bunch of hot dogs

Ralphy swears this is really how it's made. Either way, I guarantee you it's HOT! —Judy

I must have given this recipe to Ralphy—it's the same as mine! Except I add 5 tablespoons chili powder and I don't add sage! —Evelyn

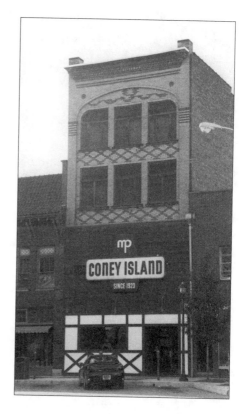

Coney Island Hot Dogs,
New Castle, Pennsylvania

Judy's Roast Pork

Boneless rolled roast pork, enough
for 4 to 6 people (ask the
butcher)
1 to 2 tablespoons salt and pepper

1 to 2 tablespoons garlic powder
1 to 2 tablespoons dried sage

Preheat oven to 350 degrees. Sprinkle salt, pepper, garlic powder, and sage to taste over roast. Rub in. Be sure to cover all sides, and don't forget the ends! Don't be afraid to use the seasonings—it's hard to use too much.

Place roast in 9 × 13-inch baking pan. Roast 45 to 50 minutes per pound, until the inside temperature of the meat is 185 degrees. Remove to plate, cover, and keep warm.

Gravy

First, make a thickening: stir together approximately ½ cup flour and enough water to make a creamy paste—not too thick, you want to be able to pour it.

Then, scrape the drippings from the baking pan into a saucepan. Add about 1 to 2 cups water and salt and pepper to taste. Keep burner at medium-high and add thickening, stirring constantly. As the mixture comes to a boil, it will get thicker. Voila! Gravy!

♦ *Serves* four to six

Kate's Shrimp Risotto

I made this for my friend Shelly's birthday a few years ago. It was delicious and not hard at all—especially since I had the guest stirring the whole time!   —Kate

1 quart chicken broth

1 ½ cups water, more if needed

1 bunch asparagus, trimmed and
   cut into 1-inch pieces

3 tablespoons cooking oil, divided

1 small onion, chopped

1 ½ cups Arborio rice, uncooked

½ cup dry white wine

1 ¼ teaspoons salt

½ pound shrimp, shelled and
   deveined, and sautéed until opaque

1 teaspoon grated zest from ½ orange

4 cloves garlic, minced

¼ cup chopped parsley

¼ teaspoon fresh-ground black
   pepper

Bring broth and water to a simmer in a medium pot. Cook asparagus in the broth until just done, about 4 minutes. Remove with a slotted spoon. Put in colander, rinse with cold water, and drain. Keep broth at a simmer.

In a large pot, heat 2 tablespoons oil. Add onion and cook, stirring occasionally, until translucent, about 5 minutes. Add rice and stir until it begins to turn opaque, about 2 minutes.

Add wine and salt. Cook, stirring, until wine is absorbed. Add about ½ cup of the simmering broth; cook, stirring frequently, until liquid is absorbed. The rice and broth should bubble gently; adjust the heat as needed. Continue cooking, adding broth ½ cup at a time and letting the rice absorb it before adding more. Cook the rice in this way until tender, about 25 to 30 minutes total. The starch from the rice should thicken the broth that isn't absorbed. You may not need all of the liquid, or you may need more broth or water.

Stir in the asparagus, shrimp, orange zest, garlic, parsley, pepper, and the remaining 1 tablespoon oil. Cook until heated through.

♦ *Serves* four

Judy's Grilled Fish in Foil

4 fish filets, fresh or frozen

2 green peppers, seeded and
    chopped

2 onions, chopped

¼ cup margarine, melted

2 tablespoons lemon juice

2 teaspoons salt

1 teaspoon paprika

Pepper to taste

Cut heavy-duty aluminum foil into four 12 × 12-inch pieces. Grease lightly.
Place 1 fish filet skin-side-down on each piece of foil. Top each with one-
quarter of the green pepper and onion. Combine remaining ingredients and
pour evenly over fish. Bring foil up and over, and close all edges. Place foil
packages on grill about 5 inches from moderately hot coals. Cook until fish
flakes easily when tested with fork (about 5 minutes).

◆ *Serves* four

Easy! Easy! Easy! —*Judy*

Grandma's Fish Oreganato

3 pounds perch, haddock, or
   flounder
½ cup olive oil
⅓ cup vinegar
½ cup finely chopped parsley
3 or 4 cloves garlic, minced

2 tablespoons dried oregano
Salt to taste
Pepper to taste
A few cups bread crumbs, coarsely
   broken

Heat oven to 375 degrees. Lay out fish on greased baking sheets or oven-proof platters. Sprinkle oil over fish, then vinegar (a little less vinegar than oil, reserving small amount of each to sprinkle before baking). Sprinkle half of parsley over fish. Sprinkle garlic, then half amount each of oregano, salt, and pepper. Top fish with bread crumbs and remaining parsley, and then the remaining oregano, salt, and pepper. Sprinkle again with rest of oil and vinegar. Bake 15 to 20 minutes.

♦ *Serves* six to eight

Joe's Swordfish with Ginger and Lemongrass

1 kaffir lime with leaf (try finding one of these in an Asian or international market—I've also used a regular grated lime peel and it worked fine)

3 tablespoons kosher salt

5 tablespoons light brown sugar

4 swordfish steaks (about 8 ounces each)

1 lemongrass stalk, sliced

1 1-inch piece fresh ginger, cut into matchsticks

1 lime

1 tablespoon peanut oil

1 large ripe avocado, peeled and pitted

1. If using the lime leaf, bruise it by crushing lightly to release the flavor. This is used primarily for the intense aroma it produces.

2. To make the marinade, process the lime leaf (or grated lime peel), kosher salt, and brown sugar in a food processor or blender until thoroughly blended.

3. Place the swordfish steaks in a bowl. Sprinkle marinade over them and add the lemongrass and ginger. Set aside in the refrigerator for 3 to 4 hours.

4. After marinating, rinse marinade off the fish and pat dry. Peel the lime. Remove any excess pith (the white part) from the peel. Cut the peel into very thin strips. Squeeze and reserve the lime juice from the fruit. Heat the wok. Add the peanut oil. When hot, add the lime peel, then the swordfish. Stir-fry for 3 to 4 minutes. Add the lime juice. Remove the wok from the heat. Slice the avocado and add to the fish. Season to taste and serve.

◆ *Serves* **four**

I've made this with amberjack steaks instead of swordfish. Tuna should be good too. —Joe

The Vegetarian in the Family

by Janice Aubrey Shoup

I became a vegetarian in 1976. Until then, my family had enjoyed all of the delicious foods and pastries and desserts I had learned in Mom's kitchen, and that meant that we enjoyed plenty of meat dishes. Rosemary chicken and potatoes, fried pork chops with garlic and parsley, and meatballs and spaghetti sauce almost as good as hers, if I do say so myself. I could make a mean braciole and had even learned how to mix together the hot sausage that Mom and Pop prepared every winter. I can still remember how they used to hang it on a makeshift rack in that cold pantry off the kitchen in our old house.

Anyhow, I had to say good-bye to all those good things, and, to make it more difficult, I had to let garlic go as well. It's funny, though. Mom never minded much that I gave up meat, but to not eat garlic ... unthinkable! Pizza without garlic? Fried peppers without garlic? Savoy cabbage and beans without garlic? Stuffed artichokes without garlic? Oh, the lectures I got! But I stuck to my guns, and when I went to visit and had to do the cooking, I wouldn't use garlic when I cooked. So to make a point, before eating my food, she would make quite a production of sprinkling on the garlic salt or- sometimes she would even go so far as to chop up garlic at the table and sprinkle it on top of her food.

Naturally I had acquired plenty of great new vegetarian recipes, but there was no way I would give up the old standbys that I had learned from Mom. There were plenty of her other tasty recipes that lent themselves to a vegetarian kitchen, and when you come down to it, southern Italian cooking is not all that meat heavy. Many of the recipes we'd grown up with featured vegetables and/or beans, and since I love them both, that was just fine with me.

The spaghetti sauce was the first hurdle. No problem. Just eliminated the garlic, added lots of nice sweet onions and much more basil. (Mom even liked it!) Other recipes, such as cabbage and beans, stuffed peppers, coogootz, pasta fazool, fried peppers, and eggplant parmigiana, weren't so hard to convert to my tastes. The only thing I changed with these recipes was to make fewer vegetables than Mom liked and to use onions instead of garlic.

Mom was a great cooking teacher, and she loved showing us her ways of doing things. Each time I fix one of Mom's recipes, I strive to make things taste as much like hers as possible. I have always done this, not because I wanted her approval (fat chance!) but because I really loved the way she cooked and I wanted to make sure I would be able to enjoy it always.

Watching her cook and eating her delicious food certainly honed my ability to taste and season food—meat or no meat. But the most important lesson she seems to have taught was how to stir her love for her family into whatever she cooked or baked, and that has to have been her true legacy. She did that because, as anyone who knew Mom knows, she couldn't easily dole out affectionate hugs or give us kisses or offer supportive encouragement. It wasn't her style. Whether she knew it or not, it was love when she stirred her polenta for Pop on his birthday, or meticulously spread those tomatoes oh-so-evenly on her pizza, or baked those bushels of delicious cookies at Christmas time, or stayed up all night waiting for the annual Easter bread to finally rise so she could bake it at just the right moment. Who needed to hear "I love you" when you could enjoy food like that?

Grandma's Stuffed Artichokes

I had the pleasure of spending a week with Grandma and Aunt Anita in 1997 so I could learn a few things about cooking. We made stuffed artichokes, my favorite Grandma recipe, among many other things. Here's what I learned from the master, herself.   —Kate

How to buy a good artichoke: You want one that isn't too big, or it will take forever to cook; make sure you hear a squeak when you squeeze them and the leaves rub together; and make sure they're not too brown on the leaves.

It's a big pain to make these. But they're so good; that's the problem.   —Grandma

4 or 5 medium artichokes

4 or 5 cups bread crumbs from day-old bread (one cup per artichoke)

3 cloves garlic, minced

½ cup olive oil, plus some more

Celery leaves, chopped

Small bunch parsley, chopped

¼ cup Romano cheese

1 to 2 eggs

Salt and pepper to taste

Handful of raisins, cut up

Stems of artichokes, washed and scraped, cut up fine

1. Start by "taking off the small leaves that aren't good for anything," as Grandma said. Clean the bottoms of the artichokes off and cut off the stems so the artichokes can sit up and not fall over. Never throw the leaves down the disposal.

Grandma removes the smaller leaves and dices stems for sautéeing.

2. Trim the stems down to the center, unless they're "Ayyyy . . . too dry and no good," in which case throw them away after complaining about them a lot. Once the stems are trimmed to the tender part, chop them and set them aside.

3. Trim dry ends of all the leaves with scissors, snipping each one straight across.

4. Slam top of artichokes against the counter hard, so that the leaves open up.

5. Pull out the fuzzy center of the artichokes. If they're really stuck in there, tools such as knives, bottle openers, scissors, and pliers can help.

6. Rinse the artichokes and drain them upside down.

Stuffing

1. Use really dry bread that you've had in your garage for weeks that must be broken with rolling pin to get crumbs. Add a little water if it's too hard to break up.

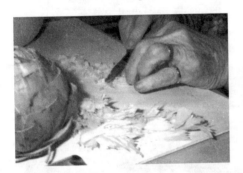

Chop celery leaves real small.

2. Sauté chopped artichoke stems with 1 clove minced garlic in olive oil that covers bottom of small skillet. When golden brown (not too brown and crunchy), turn off burner. Add to stuffing when cool.

3. Chop and add celery leaves (don't cut any of it too thick or it won't cook—cut it as small as you can), parsley, and remaining garlic.

4. Add cheese, eggs, salt, pepper, and raisins (if raisins are hard, boil in enough water to cover). Mix.

5. When the stuffing is all mixed, add a little oil to help hold together. Then separate stuffing into as many blobs as you have artichokes. This way you will have the same amount of stuffing for every artichoke.

I never liked the artichokes—it was always the stuffing.   —Grandma

Stuffing and Cooking

1. Stuff the center of the artichoke first.

2. Then stick your fingers in and pull back leaves for stuffing. Add stuffing to as many leaves as you can.

3. When all the artichokes are stuffed, arrange them in a pan. The pan should be just a little taller than the artichokes.

4. Pour a glass of water in, about 1 cup.

5. Look in the pan to see if there's enough.

6. Add another glass of water.

Divide stuffing into as many lumps as you have artichokes.

7. Add olive oil. How much? "When I say. Not now . . . not now . . . not now . . . hmmm . . . NOW!" There should be enough liquid at the bottom to come up about ¼ of the way up the side of the artichoke.

8. Add salt and pepper.

9. Make sure there's room enough for a spoon to fit between the artichokes. Or a baster. If it seems tight, don't worry—the artichokes will shrink when you cook them.

10. Cover pan and bring liquid to a boil over high heat. Reduce heat to low and monitor the pan for the next few hours to make sure there is enough oil and water in the bottom. Add more of both if needed. Baste regularly throughout cooking time.

Start by stuffing choke in the middle and work your way out.

Artichokes can be cooked in a deep pot or lower-edge pan. Leave enough room between chokes for basting.

11. Test to see if artichokes are finished by pulling out an inner leaf and tasting it —if it comes off easily and tastes good, it's done. If not, baste, cover, and continue to cook.

• *Serves* four (or eight if you split in half to serve)

Out of all the things I know how to make, I love these best.

The long cooking and basting is the secret to making them real tasty.

Nobody cooks artichokes like my mother. I try, I try. But she made the best artichokes. They used to smell so good! —Grandma

Jody and Joe show how they can prepare chokes too, with a variety of household tools.

Grandma's Eggplant Parmigiana

This recipe is based on a demonstration from Grandma. It's what I used for the huge batch I made for Grandma and Grandpa's 65th wedding anniversary.   —Anita

1 to 2 large eggplants, peeled

Salt to taste

Flour for dredging

3 eggs

1 tablespoon cracker meal

½ cup olive oil

2 to 4 cups marinara or other pasta sauce, depending on size of eggplant

2 to 3 cups grated Parmesan cheese, depending on size of eggplant

Preheat oven to 350 degrees. Slice eggplant about ¼-inch thick. Put flour and salt in paper or plastic bag, add eggplant and shake slices to dust with flour. Shake and remove excess flour and lay slices flat. Beat eggs, stir in cracker meal. Drop eggplant slices in egg mixture to coat. Heat oil and fry eggplant slices a few at a time until brown on both sides and drain on brown paper bag. Replenish oil as needed. Cover bottom of 1- or 1½-quart casserole with sauce and arrange cooked eggplant slices over sauce, overlapping as necessary to form a layer. Top with some sauce, then a handful of grated cheese. Continue layering with sauce, eggplant, and grated cheese. Bake until heated through, about 20 to 30 minutes.

♦ *Serves* six

VARIATION

For a denser casserole, salt eggplant after slicing, drain in colander for an hour, rinse, and dry. Then proceed with recipe. The eggplant slices will be thinner and layers will be closer.

Grandma's Coogootz

"Coogootz" is a dialectal derivative of the Italian word "cocozza," which is a form of summer squash, or "zucca" or "zucchini."

1 chopped onion

1 unpeeled zucchini, sliced

¼ cup olive oil, or more—enough to cover bottom of pan

1 to 2 8-ounce cans tomato sauce or pureed tomatoes

Handful of celery leaves, chopped

Handful of parsley, chopped

Basil to taste

Salt to taste

Pepper to taste

1 or 2 fresh tomatoes (optional)

1 15-ounce can pork and beans

Fry onion with zucchini in oil. Fry halfway and add pureed tomatoes. Flavor with celery leaves, parsley, basil, salt, and pepper to taste. Simmer until tender; stir regularly. Add a little water if too dry. Add fresh tomatoes if you have some on hand. Add pork and beans. Stir off the heat and see if you like how it tastes. Adjust seasonings if needed.

• *Serves* six to eight

I always add a little sugar if the tomatoes are too sour, but that's why I started to put in the pork and beans. —Grandma

Evelyn's Coogootz

Since this is a family favorite, there are probably about ten different variations of the recipe floating around. These two use Italian sausages, which makes it spicier and more filling!

2 tablespoons oil

1 ½ pounds Italian sausage, cut into ½-inch pieces

1 large onion, diced

5 small zucchini, cut into ¼-inch slices

Salt and pepper to taste

2 cups fresh crushed tomatoes or 1 28-ounce can tomato sauce

3 tender celery stalks and leaves, chopped

Basil to taste

Fennel seeds to taste

1 15-ounce can pork and beans

1. In large pot, heat oil; brown sausage. Remove and place aside. Add onion and zucchini to pan and sauté.

2. Add salt, pepper, and tomatoes. Then add celery stalks and leaves, basil, and fennel seeds to taste. Add sausage after 5 minutes.

3. Cook for 10 more minutes, giving ingredients a chance to blend. In the last 5 minutes of cooking add pork and beans.

♦ *Serves* four

GLENN'S VARIATION

The most important thing to remember is that this is a liberal recipe as far as amounts and types of contents. It almost always comes out right.

I use a bunch of small zucchinis, pork and beans, a 24-ounce can of peeled tomatoes, onions, garlic, and Italian sausage. Some "gootzophiles" also use chopped celery.

Basically, you brown onions and garlic in oil. Brown sausage at the same time and pour off excess oil. Cut zukes into small chunks, whatever shape you choose. Throw 'em in there with the onions, etc. Open the can of tomatoes and squish 'em into the mix making lots of small chunks. Pour in tomato juice from can. Add a similar size can of pork and beans. Throw sausage in at this point too, and add garlic (a lot if you're sick like me!). Add salt and pepper and bring medley to a mild boil, stirring constantly with a bottom-to-top motion. Cook until zukes are soft, about a ½ hour. Serve with fresh Italian bread.

Kate's Spinach and Beans

1 to 2 cloves garlic, chopped

Pinch salt

2 cups plain low-fat yogurt

2 tablespoons tahini

2 cups basmati rice

2 tablespoons olive oil

2½ cups hot water

1 large onion, chopped

2 additional tablespoons olive oil

1 teaspoon ground coriander

4 large bunches fresh spinach, coarsely chopped

1 14- to 16-ounce can chick peas

Salt and pepper to taste

1 bunch parsley, finely chopped

½ cup pine nuts

Combine garlic, salt, yogurt, and tahini. Set aside.

Rinse rice and soak in cold water 10 minutes. Drain. In medium saucepan, heat oil. Add rice and cook 1 minute. Add hot water and bring to a boil. Cover and reduce heat to medium-low. Simmer 30 minutes, until rice is tender.

In a large pot, sauté onion in remaining oil for 7 minutes. Add coriander, then chick peas, then stir in spinach. When spinach is wilted, add chick peas, salt, and pepper. Cover and simmer 20 minutes.

Brown pine nuts in pan over medium heat. Do not burn!

To assemble, place rice on bottom of serving dish. Then put spinach over rice and cover with yogurt mixture. Sprinkle with parsley and pine nuts.

◆ *Serves* four to six

Janice's Bulgur Wheat and Lentil Pilaf

This is one of my very favorite quickie dishes. It's really easy and tastes pretty damn good to me. I suppose some of you carnivorous types will end up sticking in some hamburger or sausage or something. That's your problem!   —Janice

1 cup lentils

2 cups water

2 cups vegetable stock (or chicken stock)

1 cup uncooked bulgur wheat

1 teaspoon salt (go easy on the salt if the broth is already salted)

Pepper to taste

1 large onion, coarsely chopped

¼ cup olive oil

Sliced raw carrots (lots)

Additional salt and pepper to taste

1. Put lentils in the water, bring to a boil, and simmer for 10 minutes; drain immediately and set aside.

2. Put stock in a saucepan, bring to a boil, and add the bulgur wheat, salt, and pepper, and bring to a boil again. Simmer, covered, for 20 minutes (or until liquid is absorbed).

3. Sauté onion in oil, then add the carrots. Brown them very quickly and then add a bit of water and cover tightly to steam over a low heat (about 10 minutes).

4. Add the bulgur mixture and cooked lentils to the onion and carrot mixture and season. Heat a little longer until flavors blend.

• *Serves* two or three hungry vegetarians, or four if meat is served with this dish

This is great with a green salad. Last time I fixed this for Roxanne, she ate her first dish with lots of freshly ground black pepper. Then, for her second dish, she poured some tamari sauce over it and loved it even more! Trust me—this is both nutritious and good (cheap, too!).   —Janice

Alexis's Cabbage and Beans

⅛ cup olive oil (or canola)

½ clove garlic, crushed (optional)

1 small or medium onion, chopped

1 head savoy cabbage, chopped into big pieces

½ cup water (more or less)

¼ cup seasoned white vinegar—find some spicy stuff if possible

1 tablespoon, more or less, spicy hot sauce

Salt and pepper to taste

1 15-ounce can cannellini beans (or two, depending on taste)

Cover bottom of heavy, large saucepan with oil. Heat oil. Brown garlic lightly and then add onion and soften. Add chopped cabbage and water, vinegar, hot sauce, salt, and pepper. You can add any spices you like that you feel would work with a cabbage dish. Cover with lid, reduce heat to slow simmer, and steam for a while, 15 minutes, maybe more. Get the cabbage soft and stir occasionally.

When all is nice and soft, add the beans and stir gently so the beans don't get smooshed up.

Eat immediately or serve later, or the next day. Add LOTS AND LOTS of stinky cheese (Parmesan, Romano, etc.). Grind some fresh pepper on top too. You can also serve over rice, if you have some leftover in the fridge.

♦ *Serves* four to six

I recommend eating four or five bowls in one sitting, if your bowels can handle it.   —Alexis

Note: This is based on one of Grandma's traditional dishes. She used dried red pepper flakes instead of hot sauce, great northern beans instead of cannellinis, and no vinegar.

GRANDPA'S BIRTHDAY

When Grandma and Grandpa were first married, and it was Grandpa's first birthday as a married man, he spent the day working at Great Grandma DeMasi's, outside in the bitter cold. Grandma, in an effort to feed her hard-working husband a nourishing and heartwarming meal, made polenta for dinner that night. Grandpa, upset that he was served such an ordinary meal for his birthday, complained, "Is this all I get for my birthday dinner?" Somehow they ended up laughing about it, and the next year, on purpose, Grandma did it again. And they laughed again, and it became a tradition. On Grandpa's birthday, everyone ate polenta.

Grandma's Polenta

Grandma and I put this together when she did a recipe scrapbook for someone once—i.e., Grandma explained and I typed it into the computer. —Anita

8 cups water

4 cloves garlic, chopped

½ cup olive or vegetable oil

1 15-ounce can great northern beans, drained

Pinch red pepper flakes (optional)

Salt and pepper to taste

2 cups yellow cornmeal

2 cups cold water (not for boiling)

1 teaspoon salt

1. Boil 8 cups of water.

2. In skillet, lightly brown garlic in oil. Add beans, red pepper flakes, salt, and pepper. Set aside.

3. Mix cornmeal in 2 cups cold water. It should be of pouring consistency. As water boils, slowly pour cornmeal into it, stirring constantly. Continue to stir until mixture thickens. Lower heat.

4. Transfer bean mixture to the polenta and cook about 10 more minutes, continuing to stir. Pour into a platter, skillet, loaf pan, or other container for serving. Mixture will get firm and can be sliced. Cut into chunks to reheat in microwave or skillet. May be topped with maple syrup or served with sausage, as described below.

To serve with sausage topping: Use 1 pound loose Italian sausage, or chop stuffed sausage into pieces. Brown in about 2 tablespoons oil. Stir in 2½ cups crushed tomatoes or tomato sauce, or a bottled sauce. Simmer 20 to 30 minutes. Sauce may be used as a topping for polenta. Sprinkle with grated cheese of choice.

To make it more special, put a layer of polenta in a dish that can be reheated. Pour on sauce. Add another layer of the polenta to the dish and top with more sauce. Reheat in oven at 350 degrees. Sprinkle with cheese.

♦ *Serves* six to eight

Casper Polenta

This is a recipe I created to celebrate the birth of my beautiful, intelligent, charming grandson, Casper Aubrey Molina.   —Janice

Polenta

2 cups cornmeal

1 cup water

2 teaspoons salt

5 cups boiling water

4 tablespoons butter

1 cup grated Parmesan

1 15-ounce can great northern
   beans, drained

Ground black pepper to taste

Sauce

1 onion, chopped

1 to 2 tablespoons olive oil

Dash red pepper flakes

1 15-ounce can whole tomatoes
   (squished or cut into small
   pieces)

1 teaspoon dried basil

½ teaspoon dried oregano

½ teaspoon dried rosemary

1 teaspoon dried marjoram

Salt, pepper, and sugar to taste

Other

3 medium-sized potatoes, peeled
   and cubed

1 to 2 tablespoons olive oil

2 green zucchinis, sliced or cubed

2 yellow zucchinis, sliced or cubed

1 onion, chopped

For polenta, whisk together cornmeal with water and salt. Stir slowly into about 5 cups boiling water and stir. Add more liquid if needed. When right consistency, stir in butter, Parmesan cheese, and beans. Add pepper to taste.

For sauce, sauté onion in oil. Sprinkle in red pepper flakes, then add tomatoes. Season with basil, oregano, rosemary, and marjoram. Add additional salt, pepper, and sugar to taste.

While making the sauce, sauté potatoes in oil. When they begin to soften, add zucchinis and onion. When they are almost done, add tomato mixture and any other vegetables you want. (I've added frozen or cooked fresh cut-up string beans before—the more veggies the better, I say!)

So plop some polenta in a dish, pour on the veggie/tomato mixture, sprinkle with some more Parmesan cheese and/or ground black pepper, and welcome to Vegetarian Heaven!

◆ *Serves* four to five

POLENTA LASAGNA

I make a type of lasagna with the first part of this recipe by spreading the polenta flat onto one or two cookie sheets, cutting out circles (with a glass) and layering it into a lasagna pan (sauce on the bottom first) like I was going to make regular lasagna. I use ricotta, spinach, Parmesan, and red sauce between the layers of the polenta (finishing with the polenta covered with sauce and Parmesan, of course), and then bake at 350 degrees for 30 minutes.

◆ *Serves* six to eight

Beck's Super Easy Quesadillas

2 tortillas per quesadilla (six to
eight total)

1 15-ounce can black beans,
drained

1 8-ounce package cheese
(something shredded, like
Cheddar)

Optional: tomatoes, onions,
anything else you like
Light sour cream as desired

Put one tortilla in nonstick pan. Open can of black beans and spoon onto tortilla. Sprinkle cheese on top. Sprinkle a little more cheese on top. Make sure you have enough cheese. Put second tortilla on top. Turn on burner to medium. Allow to cook. Once cheese is melting and bottom is getting golden brown, flip. Try your best not to spill all the beans.* Then eat the beans you did spill, while waiting for the other side to brown. Remove from stove, cut, serve with light sour cream and fresh vegetables of your choice.

♦ Makes three to four quesadillas, two to four pieces per quesadilla

*Some might argue that it is easier to smush the black beans onto the tortilla so that they will not spill when flipped. I believe that's cheating. —Beck

Janice's Spanish Rice

Of all the recipes in this book, I think THIS one has been asked about by the contributors the most. "Do you have Janice's Spanish Rice?" "How about Janice's Spanish Rice?" "You better make sure you've got Janice's Spanish Rice in there!" Pipe down! Here it is . . .   —Kate

1 medium onion, chopped

3 to 4 stalks celery, chopped

1 large red pepper, seeded and
    chopped

2 tablespoons olive oil, more if
    needed

1 to 1½ cups rice

3 8-ounce cans tomato sauce (or
    1 16-ounce can whole tomatoes,
    cut up, and 1 8-ounce can
    tomato sauce)

Salt and pepper to taste

Dried basil to taste

1 teaspoon prepared mustard

1 teaspoon or more sugar

1 15-ounce can corn, undrained

1 15-ounce can kidney beans,
    undrained

1. Brown onion, celery, and red pepper in oil. Add raw rice and brown it a bit.

2. Add tomato sauce. Fill each can with water and add to rice. Add another 1 or 2 cups of liquid as needed (depends on how much rice you use).

3. Season with salt, pepper, basil, mustard, and sugar.

4. When rice has absorbed a lot of the liquid and has cooked, add corn and kidney beans. Cook until heated through.

• *Serves* six to eight

Mrs. Sebastiani's Malfatti from Anita

This dish is also known as ravioli malfatti (badly made ravioli) or ravioli nudi (naked ravioli) because no pasta encloses the spinach "filling." Sometimes made with ricotta cheese.   —Anita

2 10-ounce packages fresh spinach
   or 3 packages frozen, chopped

½ loaf crusty Italian bread (or
   substitute 2 cups crumbs)

Hot water to moisten bread, about
   ½ cup

1 onion, finely chopped

1 clove garlic, finely chopped

2 tablespoons olive oil

1 cup dry bread crumbs

1 cup grated Parmesan cheese

½ cup chopped parsley

Salt to taste

¼ teaspoon black pepper

1 teaspoon dried basil

4 eggs, lightly beaten

3 cups hot tomato sauce

Flour for flouring hands

Additional grated Parmesan
   cheese

1. Cook the fresh spinach in the water that clings to the leaves after washing, or cook the frozen spinach according to package instructions. Drain, squeezing out as much water as possible, and chop.

2. Wet bread with enough water to crumble it.

3. Sauté onion and garlic in the oil until tender. Mix spinach, soaked bread, sautéed onion, and garlic and put through the finest blade of a meat grinder (or use food processor) and place in mixing bowl.

4. Add dry bread crumbs, cheese, parsley, salt, pepper, and basil to bowl containing processed spinach mixture. Stir in eggs.

5. Grease a baking dish for cooked malfatti and spread a small amount of tomato sauce on the bottom.

6. With lightly floured hands, shape the spinach mixture into sausage-like links (about a tablespoon each).

Line up the cooked nudi links in a greased dish, just so.

7. Drop the links, a few at a time, into a kettle of boiling salted water. Reduce the heat to let the water barely simmer and cook until the malfatti float to the surface. Remove with a slotted spoon, drain, and place in the prepared baking dish.

8. Spoon the tomato sauce over the links, sprinkle with cheese. Bake or broil to reheat. (This dish can be made a day ahead and then reheated.)

◆ *Makes* about twenty-eight malfatti, or six to eight servings

WHEN JUDY MARRIED JODY

as told to Kate DeVivo by Judy DeVivo

My family recipes are very different from Jody's. When we got married, I spent a lot of time with Grandma learning some new Italian recipes to add to my collection.

I grew up with my grandparents and mother. My mother's family were from Delaware originally, and I lived in Washington, D.C., and the cooking style I grew up with is what some might call American farm cooking, or maybe even a little Pennsylvania Dutch. Some of my favorite recipes I can remember my Grandmother Megee, G.G., making were fried tomatoes with pink gravy, leg of lamb, succotash, apple brown Betty, and bread pudding. We would have Sunday dinners each week, and my grandmother would cook big meals, usually roasts, hams, or lamb, and then we'd use the leftovers in some form or another throughout the week, in pot pies or sandwiches, for example. Sometimes we'd pick cherries from the tree outside and make homemade cherry pie. G.G.'s sister, Aunt Delma, raised chickens and turkeys on a farm in Delaware. When we visited they would cook them up and serve them along with fried parsnips, wilted spinach salad, and homemade angel food cake, with bitter

chocolate frosting and homemade ice cream. My other grandmother also cooked in the same style and served a lot of game, because my grandfather was a hunter. We had squirrel, venison, and rabbit stew—one of my favorites. I still make her vegetable soup, which is very similar to Jody's mother's minestrone. Grandma DeVivo used beans, and my grandmother used barley.

Throughout the years, I've combined a lot of the recipes I learned from my family with ones I learned from Grandma DeVivo. Creamed eggs on toast is one that I remember G.G. making during winter when it was cold. It's an old American recipe that goes back more than 100 years, and it was one of my original comfort foods!

G. G.'s Creamed Eggs on Toast

½ cup butter

6 tablespoons flour

1 quart milk

1½ teaspoons salt

½ teaspoon paprika

⅛ teaspoon pepper

¼ teaspoon hot sauce

2 teaspoons grated onion

12 eggs, hardboiled and cut up

Melt butter. Add flour, stir. Add milk. Cook till mixture thickens. Add remaining ingredients and cook until heated through. Serve over toast. Can also be served over biscuits, rice, potatoes, broccoli, or asparagus, if desired.

♦ *Serves* six to eight

Grandma's Peas and Onions

1 to 1½ large onions, diced

1 15-ounce can peas

6 eggs

Black pepper to taste

1. Slice and sauté onion until tender.

2. Drain peas and add to onions.

3. Beat eggs lightly and add, stirring quickly to coat peas. Keep stirring until eggs are set. They should be well mixed, not in too large chunks.

4. Sprinkle with black pepper.

◆ *Serves* four

Note: Grandma made this more often during Lent because it was meatless, and Lent was a time for fasting from meat.

Joe's Vegetarian Moussaka

This recipe comes compliments of an ex-girlfriend. I figured the vegetarians out there might like it. —Joe

2 large eggplants, thinly sliced

6 zucchini, cut into chunks

⅔ cup olive oil, plus extra, if
   needed

1½ pounds potatoes, peeled and
   thinly sliced

2 onions, sliced

3 garlic cloves, crushed

⅔ cup dry white wine

2 14-ounce cans chopped tomatoes

2 tablespoons tomato paste

1 15-ounce can green lentils

2 teaspoons dried oregano

4 tablespoons chopped parsley

Salt and pepper to taste

2 cups feta cheese, crumbled

2½ cups béchamel sauce
   (explained in instructions):
   3 tablespoons butter
   4 tablespoons all-purpose flour
   2½ cups milk
   Salt and pepper to taste
   Nutmeg, freshly grated, to taste
   2 eggs, beaten

4 tablespoons Parmesan cheese

1. Lightly salt the eggplants and zucchini and allow to drain in colander for 30 minutes. Rinse and pat dry.

2. Heat oil until very hot and brown eggplant and zucchini in it. Remove vegetables and drain on paper towel (very important). Next, brown the potatoes in the same pan. Remove potatoes and pat dry. Add onions and garlic (with extra oil, if needed) to pan and fry until lightly brown.

3. Pour in wine and reduce. Add tomatoes, tomato paste, and lentils with lentil juice. Stir in herbs and seasonings. Cover and simmer for 15 minutes.

4. In a large ovenproof dish, layer veggies and potatoes, trickling tomato/lentil sauce in between and scattering feta cheese throughout. Finish with top layer of eggplants.

5. Cover with aluminum foil and bake at 375 degrees for 25 minutes, or until veggies are soft.

6. To make béchamel sauce, put butter, flour, and milk in saucepan and bring slowly to a boil, stirring or whisking constantly, until it thickens. Season with salt and pepper and add nutmeg.

7. Remove sauce from heat and cool for 5 minutes, then beat in eggs. Pour over layered vegetables and sprinkle with Parmesan.

8. Bake for another 25 to 30 minutes, until golden and bubbling hot.

◆ *Serves* four to six, depending on how hungry people are

Kate's Pad Thai

8 ounces uncooked rice noodles

3 tablespoons Asian fish sauce

2 to 3 tablespoons fresh lemon
   juice

4 tablespoons rice wine vinegar

2 tablespoons ketchup

4 teaspoons sugar

½ teaspoon crushed red pepper

3 tablespoons vegetable oil

1 package extra-firm tofu, cubed

2 green onions, thinly sliced

3 cloves garlic, minced

3 ounces raw small shrimp, peeled
   and deveined

2 cups fresh bean sprouts

1 egg, beaten

2 to 3 tablespoons crunchy peanut
   butter (or more, as needed)

1 medium carrot, shredded

3 tablespoons minced fresh
   cilantro

A lime or two

Place noodles in medium bowl. Cover with lukewarm water and let stand 30 minutes, or until soft. Drain and set aside. Whisk together fish sauce, lemon juice, rice wine vinegar, ketchup, sugar, and crushed red pepper in small bowl; set aside.

Heat oil in large nonstick skillet over medium-high heat. Add tofu, green onions, and garlic and cook for a few minutes. Stir in shrimp and cook until opaque. Add noodles; cook 1 minute. Add bean sprouts and egg, making sure egg is cooked all the way through before moving on to next step. Stir in fish sauce mixture; toss to coat evenly. Add peanut butter until it is peanutty enough for your taste. Cook until heated through.

Arrange noodle mixture on platter; sprinkle with carrot and cilantro. Squeeze with lime wedges before eating.

♦ *Serves* four

Side Dishes

- Judy's Marinated Carrots
- Anita's Mustard Carrots
- Judy's Sauerkraut
- Grandma's Greens and Beans
- Anita's Sweet Potatoes Rosemary
- Aunt Jane's Sweet Potato-Marshmallow Casserole
- Rose's Broccoli-Corn Bake
- Roxanne's Fried Potatoes
- Alexis's Mac and Cheese
- Grandma's Fried Pumpkin Flowers
- Pizza Fritte
- Janice's Onion Pie
- Evelyn's Fried Peppers
- An Ode to Fried Peppers
- Rose's Zucchini Casserole
- Grandma's Pickled Eggplant
- Judy's Asparagus/Tomato Salad
- Debbie's Asian Slaw
- Judy's Cucumbers in Sour Cream
- Mrs. Aubrey's Pineapple Cream Cheese Salad
- G.G.'s Orange-Carrot-Pineapple Salad

- Judy's Waldorf Salad
- Evelyn's Bean Salads 1 and 2
- Curt's Shopska Salad
- Marjory Mariner's Best Pasta Salad
- Beck's Favorite Pasta Salad
- Kate's 4th of July Pasta Salad
- Grandma's Hot Chicken Salad
- Codfish Salad
- Evelyn's Mushrooms in Tomato Sauce
- Debbie's Oriental Chicken Salad
- Kate's Fruit Slaw
- Basic Italian Red Onion and Orange Salad
- Jody's Dinner Salad

Judy's Marinated Carrots

1 pound of baby carrots

3 tablespoons olive oil

2 tablespoons white vinegar

Pinch sugar and salt

¼ teaspoon dried oregano

2 tablespoons crushed garlic

1. Cut carrots into strips and boil for 8 minutes.

2. Mix olive oil, white vinegar, sugar, salt, oregano, and garlic.

3. Pour oil mixture over carrots, making sure to cover them all.

4. Marinate in refrigerator 6 to 8 hours, or overnight, before serving.

♦ *Serves* ten to twelve as appetizer, six to eight as side dish

Anita's Mustard Carrots

3 pounds carrots, peeled
½ cup water
4 tablespoons butter
½ cup brown sugar

¼ cup mustard
2 tablespoons chopped chives
2 tablespoons chopped parsley

1. Simmer and drain carrots. Cut into chunks.

2. Combine butter, brown sugar, and mustard, and cook until butter and sugar are melted.

3. Pour mixture over cooked carrots.

4. When ready to serve, sprinkle chives and parsley over the carrots and mix in.

• *Serves* four to six

Judy's Sauerkraut

1 32-ounce bag sauerkraut

1 to 2 links Italian sausage (hot or
  mild), cooked

1 tablespoon butter

1 apple, chopped into small pieces

1 small onion, chopped

Salt and pepper to taste

Remove sauerkraut from bag and rinse in colander. Dice sausage. In skillet, melt butter. Add apple and onion, cook until onion is limp. Add sausage. Cook 1 minute more. Add sauerkraut. Mix all together, add salt and pepper to taste. Put into 2-quart casserole. Bake at 350 degrees till heated through.

♦ *Serves* eight to ten

Grandma's Greens and Beans

This is a dish I hated as a child but learned to love. When cooking Greens and Beans in large quantities, there are often leftovers. My mother took advantage of this often when she ran out of ideas for feeding her family. In her resourceful way, she would tear day-old bread into bite-size pieces, add them to the leftover greens so that the bread would be moist but not wet and cook in an oiled skillet. If it was too dry, she would add a little water or a bit of broth and mix until the bread and greens were well blended. After turning the mixture over a few times, the bread would begin to stick to the skillet, or form a light crust. Then it was time to remove the contents to a platter, sprinkle it with grated cheese and a dash of hot pepper, and serve it.   —Evelyn

1 small head cabbage, or 1 head escarole, or half of each
⅓ cup olive oil, plus some more, if necessary
3 cloves garlic, chopped

1 small onion (optional), chopped
1 15-ounce can great northern beans, undrained
Salt and pepper to taste
Pinch red pepper flakes

Prepare a large pot, half-filled with salted water, and bring to a boil. Clean and cut cabbage into bite-sized pieces, discarding stem. Clean and cut escarole, reserving tender inner leaves for salad. Cook in water until stems crush in fingers, about 10 minutes. Remove from water and drain in colander.

In another pot, lightly brown garlic and onion in oil. To prevent splattering, slowly add contents of can of beans. Add salt and pepper and simmer for 5 to 6 minutes. Add greens and mix with other ingredients. Cook together for about 15 minutes, turning often to blend the flavors. If too dry, add enough water to keep the mixture slightly soupy. Remove from heat. Covering and allowing to sit for several hours enhances the flavor of the dish.

◆ *Serves* **four to six**

Mom was budget-conscious. She bought greens when the price was right and cooked them as described in the first part of the recipe, then froze them for later use.   —Anita

Anita's Sweet Potatoes Rosemary

Sweet potatoes (at least 1 per person)

Olive oil, enough to coat each potato

Salt and pepper to taste

Garlic to taste

Dried parsley to taste

Dried rosemary to taste

Peel sweet potatoes and cut into 1-inch chunks. Add oil. Add salt, pepper, garlic, parsley, and rosemary to taste, and turn to coat on all sides. Transfer to a baking pan and bake uncovered in 350-degree oven, stirring from time to time. Remove when potatoes are fork-tender and beginning to brown, 45 minutes to 1 hour.

♦ *Servings* vary, depending on how many sweet potatoes you use

Aunt Jane's Sweet Potato-Marshmallow Casserole

3 medium-size sweet potatoes
½ cup butter
1 10-ounce package marshmallows
 (large or miniature)

Cook and skin sweet potatoes, then mash. Pat in butter until smoothly mixed.

Grease casserole and arrange alternate layers of potatoes and marshmallows. Place some marshmallows on top. Bake at 400 degrees for 10 to 15 minutes, or until nicely browned.

◆ *Serves* six

Note: Large marshmallows can also be halved, if desired.

Rose's Broccoli–Corn Bake

10 ounces frozen chopped broccoli

1 16-ounce can cream-style corn

1 egg, beaten

1 tablespoon minced onion

½ cup coarse saltine cracker
   crumbs, divided

2 tablespoons melted butter,
   divided

Salt and pepper to taste

Preheat oven to 350 degrees. Cook broccoli according to package directions and drain. Combine with corn, egg, onion, half of the cracker crumbs, half of the butter, salt, and pepper. Top with remaining cracker crumbs and butter. Bake for 30 minutes.

♦ *Serves* four to six

Roxanne's Fried Potatoes

These fried potatoes are great for breakfast or dinner. It doesn't matter. It took me years, and I mean years, before I figured out how to cook them well. I had to watch Evelyn and Grandma do it a couple of times before I got it. So, in the end, I finally realized that the potatoes have to steam to cook and have to fry for flavor. Durrrrr.   —Roxanne

These are the amounts per person:

About 1 tablespoon olive oil,
   roughly

½ small onion, chopped small

½ large clove garlic, minced

Salt and red pepper flakes
   to taste

1 large potato, quartered and
   sliced

PLUS

Glass of wine, beer, or cocktail—
   this is not a short process

Put some olive oil in a big frying pan that has a lid and is already hot. Get the oil warm, then add the onion and garlic. Then add salt and red pepper flakes. Cook for a few minutes, just enough to get the vegetables a little soft, and throw in the potatoes and start stirring them around. Heat should be on medium at this point.

The trick to cooking these things is to stir them, cover them, walk away, sit down, sip your beverage, go back, stir, cover, walk, sit, sip—over and over again, until the potatoes are cooked and there are a lot of really dark brown bits at the bottom (because these are the best parts).

Grandpa used to sneak some water into the pan to hurry the steaming process.
   —Anita

Alexis's Mac and Cheese

Here's a recipe that my mom gave me years ago, and I just tried it. I don't know why I never did before. Check this out!   —Alexis

1¼ to 1½ cups dry elbow macaroni
½ cup chopped onion (or less, if preferred)
2 tablespoons butter
3 tablespoons flour
1 15-ounce can stewed tomatoes

8 ounces American cheese, shredded
½ teaspoon mixture of dried oregano, rosemary, and basil
⅛ teaspoon garlic powder
½ teaspoon salt
Grated Parmesan cheese

Preheat oven to 350 degrees. Grease casserole dish. *(I didn't grease mine and it was easy to clean anyway.   —Alexis)* Cook and drain macaroni. Cook onion in butter. Stir in flour, then tomatoes. Thicken. Add cheese, stir until melted, then add seasonings. Put it all together in casserole. Sprinkle with Parmesan. Cook 20 minutes in oven. Yum.

◆ *Serves* two to four

I added tons of wheat germ on top, too. It's very rich, but extremely tasty—evil is the word. Took me 40 minutes start to finish.   —Alexis

ADDITIONAL VARIATIONS

Thickly chop some zucchinis and sauté with onions. This is a variation on another recipe that mom makes—it would work nicely. (I would also attempt corn . . . as I am a corn whore.)

Grandma's Fried Pumpkin Flowers

Though we referred to them as pumpkin flowers, generally it was zucchini flowers that we used. You cannot usually find them in the markets; they are most often found in home gardens for a few August weeks. They must be picked very early in the morning, on the day that they are to be served. Mix the batter and, while it rests, prepare the flowers for frying.   —Evelyn

Batter

1 cup flour

1 teaspoon baking powder

½ teaspoon salt

½ teaspoon cinnamon

1 large egg

About ½ cup (could be more or less) milk to make a runny batter, similar to consistency of pancake batter

Sift together dry ingredients. Then add egg and milk and allow to rest for 30 minutes.

Flower Prep

Try not to tear the delicate flowers after picking. Carefully rinse them, gently shake off the moisture, and place on a paper towel. Remove all leaves, gently clip the stamen and the stem, leaving a stub to hold on to when you coat it.

Frying the Flowers

To a heavy skillet, add olive oil to a depth of ¼-inch and begin to heat it to frying temperature. Meanwhile, dip each flower carefully into the batter until it is totally coated. Lightly brown on both sides. Remove flowers to drain on a paper towel until ready to serve. If batter becomes too thick, add a bit of milk until it is runny again. These are best eaten immediately after frying.

An electric skillet is preferable because the heat remains constant. If using a stove-top skillet, adjust heat so that fritters brown equally; add oil as needed. Try to keep flowers from touching each other in skillet. —Evelyn

♦ *Makes* ten to twelve fried flowers

Pizza Fritte

When Mom made bread for the family, we all knew there would be a treat that day. She always made sure there was enough leftover dough to make pizza fritte. Mangia, figlia, mia, mangia!   —Evelyn

Use your favorite bread dough recipe, thawed frozen bread dough, or this quick method:

1 package dry yeast
1½ cups warm water (110° to
    115°F) with ½ teaspoon sugar
4 cups flour
Pinch of salt

Dissolve yeast in water/sugar mixture. Add flour, 1 cup at a time, until it forms a ball.

Dough should be almost sticky. Allow to rise. Pinch off a small portion and stretch it into a small pizza shape, about the size of an adult palm. Deep-fry in hot oil, turning over once as soon as it lightly browns. Drain on paper towels. Serve hot after sprinkling with white sugar.

◆ *Serves* as many people are there—they'll eat however much you make!

Janice's Onion Pie

Here's a delicious side dish for all you meat eaters out there! You'll want to eat the whole thing all by yourself and all at one sitting! —Janice

Crust

1 cup unsalted saltine crackers,
  crushed
4 tablespoons melted butter

Filling

4 cups thinly sliced yellow onions

4 tablespoons butter

4 eggs

1 teaspoon salt

¼ teaspoon pepper

1½ cups milk

¼ cup grated Cheddar cheese

Mix saltines with 4 tablespoons melted butter to make crust. Line pie pan with mixture.

For filling, sauté onion in 4 tablespoons butter and pour into crust. Whisk together eggs with salt and pepper, then add milk and whisk together with eggs. Pour egg and milk mixture over onions. Before placing in oven, cover with grated Cheddar cheese. Bake at 350 degrees for 25 to 30 minutes. It will puff up.

♦ *Serves* six to eight as a side dish (depending on whether people have self-control)

Evelyn's Fried Peppers

1 to 2 medium green or red bell
   peppers per person
About 1 to 2 tablespoons olive oil

Garlic, sliced (1 large clove
   for every 2 or 3 peppers)
Salt and pepper to taste

Allow at least one medium pepper per serving. Wash and remove stem and seeds from each. Trim away inner membranes and imperfections. Slice lengthwise into ¼- or ½-inch slices. Sauté slices in sizzling olive oil until they begin to brown, gently stirring them as they fry. Lower heat so they don't burn. If frying a large quantity, a lid can be used to steam them for the early part of the cooking process. When peppers are tender, add sliced garlic cloves to the mix. Cook together until the garlic is slightly browned. Add salt and pepper as desired.

♦ *Servings* depend on the number of peppers you use

Some members of the family feel that the peppers are better the next day. You might have to double the recipe for this purpose.   —Evelyn

Make sure to use lots of salt and garlic—and make enough for leftovers!

An Ode to Fried Peppers

by Evelyn Meine

Recently
I came across two peppers.
    In my fridge.
They had been there a while.

I heard a voice.

It said, "Don't let those go to waste."
It said, "Stuff them or fry them or do something with
    them."
It said, "Don't let them spoil."

I had a vision.

Of an electric frying pan piled high with sliced green
    peppers.
Of little bits of garlic jumping and browning in hot oil.
Of slices of freshly baked bread
    heavy with the freshly fried and blackened peppers in
    between,
Of leftover juices being sopped up with bread chunks
    when the peppers are gone.

So
I went out and bought another pepper,
    just to be sure,
and some soft rolls

and came home and fried myself some peppers.
Turned them over and over.
Listened to the hiss and crackle.
Watched the garlic dance.
    And when they were limp and dark just right
I forked those peppers right onto the bread.

I scarfed up two whole fried pepper sandwiches.

Then I wiped up those fried pepper juices with small chunks of bread and
ate them all up, too.
Along with some good cheese and cold Coke.
Aah,
a feast fit for a queen.

And the best part was the memories:
The garage, door open to the day.
The flag.
The old picnic table with red checkered oilcloth.
Flowers in a canning jar vase.
The plants.
And, of course, Mom
slicing up green peppers for the next summer meal.

Is there anything better than a fried pepper sandwich?

Rose's Zucchini Casserole

3 cups thinly sliced zucchini
   (2 zucchini)
1 small onion, chopped
4 eggs
½ cup vegetable oil, or less
1 teaspoon chopped parsley

1 teaspoon dried basil
Salt and pepper to taste
Garlic to taste (optional)
½ cup grated Parmesan cheese
1 cup biscuit mix

Mix everything together. Pour into greased baking dish. Bake at 350 degrees for 45 minutes to 1 hour or until top is golden-brown.

• Makes about 2 dozen squares

Grandma's Pickled Eggplant

This is a recipe handwritten by Grandma around 1970. It has been edited to show the way she did it in her later years.

EGGPLANT

1 large eggplant, peeled

1 to 2 quarts salted water, or enough to cover (be generous with salt)

BRINE

½ cup white vinegar

1½ cups boiling water (or less)

SEASONINGS

1 to 2 cloves garlic, minced

Salt and pepper to taste

1 teaspoon dried oregano

Red pepper flakes (optional)

ADDITIONAL GARNISH

(ANY OR ALL)

Celery leaves, chopped

1 stalk celery, chopped

Parsley, chopped

Red and/or green vinegar peppers,* chopped

Ripe black olives, pitted and chopped

DRESSING

1 cup olive oil

Vinegar to taste

Peel eggplant and slice very thin (¼-inch slices). As slicing, drop eggplant into salted water and soak for 5 to 10 minutes. Make brine in small pot and heat to low boil. Drop eggplant into brine for a minute or two, several slices at a time. Remove with slotted spoon and put in strainer until all are done. While cooling, mix garlic, salt, pepper, oregano, red pepper flakes, and any additional garnish. When slices are cool enough to handle, squeeze out excess brine and return to a bowl. Add garlic mixture and toss, then add oil and vinegar to taste. Chill. When ready to serve, stir in more oil and vinegar to taste.

◆ Makes 1 pint to 1½ pints, depending on how large eggplant is

Anita says for less juicy relish, salt eggplant after slicing, drain in a colander for several hours, rinse off salt, and proceed with recipe. A small amount of sugar may be added to cooking vinegar to cut acid.

Aunt Julia, Grandma's sister, used to make thicker slices, almost big enough to cover a slice of homemade bread. She salted and pressed the eggplant, then, without cooking, she would layer them in a big crock with garlic, oil, and a bit of vinegar. She kept the crock in a cold cellar. When we visited, she would bring up a bowlful of these brown, leathery slices, hold a loaf of bread to her breast and cut toward herself, somehow making the bread slices all the same size. Then she made those unforgettable "sangwidges." —Anita

*See Grandma's Hot Chicken Salad, page 176, for instructions on how to make vinegar peppers.

Judy's Asparagus/Tomato Salad

1 bunch asparagus

2 tomatoes, diced

2 ounces goat cheese, crumbled

Sweet vinaigrette dressing
to lightly cover asparagus
(to taste, really)

1. Trim ends from asparagus. Steam until tender (not mushy). Let cool to room temperature.

2. Mix diced tomatoes with crumbled goat cheese.

3. On a plate, place asparagus spears on one side and tomato mixture on the other. Pour vinaigrette over all.

◆ *Serves* three to four

Debbie's Asian Slaw

4 teaspoons sesame seeds
1 cup slivered almonds
4 small green onions, finely chopped
1 package chicken-flavored ramen noodles, uncooked and broken up into small pieces

1 package fresh coleslaw, about 16 ounces
4 tablespoons red wine vinegar
1 cup vegetable oil
4 teaspoons sugar
Salt and pepper to taste
Chicken flavoring (from ramen noodles)

Toast sesame seeds and slivered almonds until slightly brown. Add onions and ramen noodles and combine with coleslaw. Set aside. Mix rest of ingredients separately to make dressing and chill. Just before serving, pour dressing over all.

♦ *Serves* about sixteen

Judy's Cucumbers in Sour Cream

2 medium cucumbers

1 teaspoon salt

1 cup sour cream

1 small red onion, thinly sliced

1½ tablespoons lemon juice

¼ cup sugar

Pepper to taste

Paprika for color

Peel and cut cucumbers in slices and sprinkle with salt. Stir to be sure salt gets through. Chill in refrigerator for 1 hour. Drain on paper towel. Mix together sour cream, onion, lemon juice, sugar, and pepper. Combine with cucumbers and sprinkle top with paprika.

◆ Serves **five to six**

If you wish, you can use vinegar instead of lemon juice. It's almost as good.
 —Judy

Mrs. Aubrey's
Pineapple Cream Cheese Salad

2 envelopes unflavored gelatin
½ cup of boiling water
1 15-ounce can of crushed
   pineapple (tall can, not flat)
½ cup sugar
Juice of half a lemon
   (2 to 3 tablespoons)

1 8-ounce package cream
   cheese
1 10-ounce bottle chopped
   maraschino cherries
   and juice
8 ounces whipped cream

1. In one bowl, dissolve gelatin and boiling water.

2. In another bowl, mix pineapple, sugar, and lemon juice and add to gelatin.

3. In another bowl, mash cream cheese and cherries. Add to gelatin, mix well, and chill until soft set.

4. When set, stir in the whipped cream until well mixed, then pour into a flat serving dish and chill until firm.

• *Serves* eight to ten

Note: Whipped topping may be substituted for whipped cream. Also, a double recipe fills a 9×13-inch dish.

G.G.'s Orange-Carrot-Pineapple Salad

2 3-ounce packages orange Jell-O

1½ to 2 cups water

1 large carrot, pared and shredded

1 10-ounce can pineapple chunks,
   drained

Prepare 1 package orange Jell-O, using 1½ cups of water and put in refrigerator. Pare and shred carrot. When Jell-O is semi-firm, stir in the carrot shreds and pineapple chunks. Let gel the rest of way in refrigerator.

◆ *Serves* six to eight

Judy's Waldorf Salad

6 to 8 apples, cut into bite-sized
   pieces (do not peel—you want
   the color!)
3 to 4 stalks celery, diced fine
1 cup dark raisins

1 cup chopped walnuts or pecans
½ cup mayonnaise (or as needed)
Lettuce leaves, washed and dried,
   to be used as bed for salad

Mix first four ingredients together. You want to add enough mayonnaise to make the salad moist, without making it dripping. Arrange lettuce leaves on plates, put apple mixture on top.

♦ *Serves* eight to ten

Evelyn's Bean Salads 1 and 2

Version 1

1 15-ounce can green beans,
   drained
1 15-ounce can red kidney beans,
   drained
1 15-ounce can garbanzo beans,
   drained
1 red onion, thinly sliced
½ cup chopped green pepper

DRESSING
½ cup oil
½ cup red wine vinegar
Dash sugar, basil, garlic, salt,
   pepper or to taste

Version 2

1 15-ounce can *each* kidney beans,
   green beans, wax beans,
   drained
1 14- or 15-ounce can artichoke
   hearts, quartered, drained
1 4-ounce can mushrooms, drained
1 7-ounce can pitted black olives,
   drained
2 cups thinly sliced celery
1 onion, thinly sliced

DRESSING
⅔ cup oil
¼ cup *each* red wine and cider
   vinegar
2 tablespoons sugar
1 teaspoon *each* dried oregano and
   salt
¼ teaspoon *each* pepper and garlic
   salt

Mix all ingredients with dressing. Marinate in refrigerator or at room temperature for several hours or overnight.

♦ *Serves* about ten (each version)

Curt's Shopska Salad

This is the national salad of Bulgaria. Hardly a lunch or dinner goes by in Bulgaria without a Shopska. Everywhere you eat in the country, your table has little bottles of oil and vinegar just waiting for the Shopska Salad to arrive. And after you work there a while you get somewhat addicted. You leave the country and you start craving it. Best thing is, there's not much to it.   —Curt

Tomatoes, 2 large or 4 small

1 cucumber

1 or 2 onions

2 peppers (optional)

1 cup sheep's milk cheese (Greek
   feta will do)

8 tablespoons olive oil
   (or vegetable oil)

2 teaspoons vinegar

2 tablespoons chopped parsley

Salt to taste

Ok. Slice and dice tomatoes and (peeled) cucumbers into small pieces. Slice your onion into thin pieces. Mix them together (though in some places they just lay them out separate in your salad plate). If you're using peppers (red are better, but green will do), it's best to roast them, removing the seeds and then cutting them into small pieces. Salt to taste. Serve the salad in individual bowls or in a larger bowl. Grate or crumble the cheese somewhat generously over the salad. Drizzle with oil and vinegar and garnish with parsley. You can add a little sliced hot pepper if you like, too.

◆ *Serves* four

Marjory Mariner's Best Pasta Salad

(WITH GRANDMA'S ADJUSTMENTS)

Marjory Mariner was a radio and cooking personality in Youngstown, Ohio.   —Evelyn

8 to 12 ounces rotini (or small
   shells or bows), cooked
3 carrots, grated
½ cup grated Romano cheese
½ cup grated American sharp
   cheese
1 cup chopped celery
3 tablespoons chopped green
   pepper
¼ cup sweet pickle relish
¼ teaspoon celery seed
Black pepper to taste

¼ cup light slaw dressing
½ cup mayonnaise
Grated onion
1 4¼-ounce can black olives,
   sliced

GARNISH

2 hardboiled eggs, sliced
Sliced tomato
Radish roses
Paprika to taste
Green onions

Mix all ingredients, chill, and garnish.

• *Serves* six to eight

I stir in about 1 tablespoon horseradish when I make this. It makes all the difference in the world!   —Evelyn

Beck's Favorite Pasta Salad

1-pound box rotini

½ cup-*ish* fresh basil

1 cup sliced mushrooms

1 cup marinated sun-dried
    tomatoes

1 cup-*ish* pine nuts

1½ packages crumbled feta cheese
    (3½ to 4 ounces)

Olive oil and balsamic vinegar
    (about three parts oil to one
    part vinegar—enough to coat)

Cook pasta. Refrigerate. Chop basil, mushrooms, and sun-dried tomatoes. Once pasta is cool, add all the rest of the ingredients except the oil and vinegar. Be generous with the feta. Use an oil and vinegar dressing. Don't over-dress. Once combined you have a tasty, and pretty, pasta salad.

◆ *Serves* eight to ten

It gets even better as the week goes on. To a point. Then it gets much worse.   —Beck

Kate's 4th of July Pasta Salad

This is a variation on a recipe my college roommate Julie taught me. She learned it from her mother, who used fat-free Italian salad dressing—it's really good!   —Kate

1 16-ounce box rotini

1 green pepper, seeded and chopped

1 red pepper, seeded and chopped

2 or 3 green onions and tops, chopped

8 radishes, chopped

2 Roma tomatoes, seeded and chopped

3 to 5 tablespoons olive oil

1 to 2 teaspoons or more vinegar

Splash of orange juice (processed), about ⅛ cup

2 cloves garlic, minced

Salt and pepper to taste

3 tablespoons fresh basil

¼ cup shredded Parmesan cheese

Cook pasta. Put into colander and stuff ice cubes throughout, while running under cool water. Once cooled and drained, add chopped veggies. Mix rest of ingredients except cheese in separate bowl, or throw it all in the blender. Pour dressing over pasta and veggies, mix, and top with cheese.

♦ Serves six to eight

Grandma's Hot Chicken Salad

Grandma usually made this dish with chicken boiled for Wedding Soup (see page 29). It's festive and great in sandwiches, kind of a chicken sloppy joe.   —Anita

1 cup sliced celery

1 large onion, chopped

½ cup olive oil

1 15-ounce can tomato puree with
    1 can water, or 4 8-ounce cans
    tomato sauce

3 to 4 vinegar peppers,* diced,
    or 2 tablespoons vinegar

1 tablespoon or more sugar

Salt and pepper to taste

½ cup sliced ripe olives or small
    can olives

1 3- to 4-pound chicken, boiled,
    skinned, and boned

Sauté celery and onion in oil until soft. Add tomatoes, vinegar peppers or vinegar, sugar, salt, pepper, and olives. Simmer thoroughly to cook celery and blend flavors. Arrange chicken on platter and top with sauce. May be reheated, also good cold.

◆ *Serves* six to eight

Vinegar peppers are made by soaking peppers in salted water for an hour. Then boil equal parts water and vinegar and cool. Drain the salted peppers and soak in vinegar water for several hours.

Codfish Salad

1 pound dried salted cod,
  presoaked (additional soaking period for 4 to 6 hours is
  recommended, changing water
  periodically to remove salt)
2 cups diced green *and* red vinegar
  peppers*
About ½ cup chopped celery leaves
  and tender stalks
About ½ cup chopped parsley
  leaves
1 15-ounce can pitted black olives,
  drained

DRESSING
¾ cup olive oil
¾ cup white wine vinegar
1 lemon, juice and grated rind
2 cloves garlic, minced
2 tablespoons dried oregano
Salt and pepper to taste

Parboil cod for 5 to 7 minutes, or until fish flakes when rubbed between the fingers. Let cool. Add peppers, celery, parsley, and olives. Mix dressing and add approximately three-quarters of the dressing to combined mixture. Refrigerate 24 hours. Before serving, add remaining dressing, if needed, to enhance flavor.

• *Serves* ten to twelve

*See previous recipe for instructions on how to make vinegar peppers.

Evelyn's Mushrooms in Tomato Sauce

2 pounds mushrooms, cut up into
    bite-size pieces
½ cup mild olive oil
1 or 2 large onions, sliced
2 cloves garlic, cut up
1 green pepper, seeded and sliced

1 28- to 30-ounce can crushed
    tomatoes
1 bay leaf
Dash cayenne pepper or hot sauce
Salt and pepper to taste
1 tablespoon sugar

Scald mushrooms by dipping into boiling water briefly and drain well. Heat oil in skillet and add onions, garlic, pepper, and scalded mushrooms. Sauté over high heat, until brown and almost crisp. Add tomatoes, bay leaf, and rest of ingredients. Cook over low heat for 20 to 25 minutes. Serve with crackers or bread.

♦ *Serves* six to eight

This can be used as a kind of side to spaghetti or fried peppers. —Evelyn

Debbie's Oriental Chicken Salad

3 chicken breasts, cooked and
chopped into small pieces
1 package coleslaw mix, about
10 ounces
4 tablespoons sliced green onions
2 tablespoons sesame seeds
1 cup slivered almonds
2 packages chicken-flavored
ramen noodles, uncooked
and crumbled

2 packages chicken flavoring
(from ramen noodles)
¼ cup sugar
2 tablespoons white wine vinegar
½ cup vegetable oil
2 tablespoons soy sauce

Mix chicken, coleslaw mix, green onions, sesame seeds, and almonds.
Toss with ramen noodles.

For the dressing, mix chicken flavoring, sugar, vinegar, oil, and soy sauce.
Toss with salad. Marinate overnight, or until noodles soften.

◆ *Serves* about sixteen

Kate's Fruit Slaw

Beck and I made this for our Mother's Day dinner and sleepover with Mom (Judy) last year . . . it was so good!   —Kate

1 tablespoon sugar

2 tablespoons fresh lime juice

1 tablespoon minced cilantro

1 tablespoon Asian fish sauce

½ tablespoon chili sauce

1 clove garlic, minced

2 cups julienned cantaloupe

1 cup julienned carrot

½ cup julienned mango

½ cup julienned Asian pear

In a bowl, dissolve the sugar in the lime juice. Stir in the cilantro, fish sauce, chili sauce, and garlic. In another bowl, combine cantaloupe, carrot, mango, and Asian pear. Add the dressing, toss, and refrigerate until cold.

• *Serves* two to four

Basic Italian Red Onion and Orange Salad

Lettuce of your choice (romaine, iceberg, Boston, mesclun, or a mixture)

½ red onion, chopped or sliced thin

1 orange, broken into bits, seeds removed

2 to 3 tablespoons olive oil

Garlic to taste

Splash red wine vinegar

Salt and pepper to taste

Seasonings to taste (dried oregano, Italian seasoning, dried basil, whatever you like)

This salad is very easy and delicious with pasta. Just throw it all together and taste as you go. The most important thing to remember is to go easy on the seasonings—the orange and red onion complement each other well and shouldn't be overshadowed by overbearing herbs.

◆ *Serves* **four to six**

Note: Grandma usually did not use onion and didn't add extra seasoning.

JODY'S DINNER SALAD

by Jody DeVivo

I finally figured out why my salads are special. It's because they're never the same. I never measure any of my ingredients, and it's amazing what a difference in taste a little more salt, or a little less vinegar, or a more liberal sprinkling of oregano can make. But, here's the thing—it all tastes good!

My ingredients are always lettuce (iceberg usually, but often times Bibb or romaine, or a mixture of whatever I have. I never cut lettuce, always tear it), onions (thin slices, never in chunks unless the whole salad is in chunks), sliced tomatoes (I hate those small ones that you have to put in your mouth whole and then they explode when you bite into them) or oranges instead of the tomatoes (try to keep out the seeds and the membranes and keep the juice. I find it's better to tear oranges into pieces rather than slice them neatly). I'd add olives more often, but Judy hates them. Radishes and celery are good occasional additions. For the dressing, I add to the salad bowl in this order: garlic cloves cut into teeny tiny pieces, salt, ground pepper, oregano, olive oil (we use the light), and red wine vinegar. If it turns out that you put in too much of anything, feel free to add water to thin it out. Oh, once or twice I used lemon juice instead of vinegar, and it tasted good, too.

---

*An excerpt from a letter
Dad once wrote to me while I was
living in Italy for a summer:*

Ciao Bambina (that means 'eat the deer'),

You should have tasted my salad tonight. I cut the lettuce into little pieces and the tomato (so you could hardly tell there was any) and the onions and green pepper. All in little pieces. Oh, I also added hearts of palm for some strange reason I can't remember. Then I did the usual dressing plus blue cheese. It was wonderful. Love, Papa

—*Kate*

◆ ◆ ◆

Desserts

- G.G.'s Baked Custard
- Anita's Lemon Ice
- Judy's Citrus Trifle
- Babs's Peach Dessert
- Aunt's Easter Bread
- Grandma's Easter Rice
- The Lamb Cake
- Debbie's Fool's Toffee
- Babs's Fudge

GLOVES:
THE COOKIE WITH 100 NAMES

This is by no means a comprehensive list, but the following are some of the other names for Gloves that Anita gave me that you might recognize.   —Kate

bow ties
bugie (little lies,
     Piedmont)
cenci (Tuscany)
chiacchere (gossips,
     Lombardy)
chuff
crofani (Tyrol)
crostoli (crusts)
dolci di Santa Lucia
farfalletti
fiocchi (Tuscany)

foglie arrostiti
frappe
fried diamond twists
fritelle piene di vento
galani
grostollie
guandi, guanti (gloves)
Italian angel wings
Italian love knots
knots
lattughe (lettuce, Emilia
     Romagna)

lingue delle suocere
(mother-in-law's
tongue)
mixed-up thoughts
nastri (ribbons)
nastri delle suore (nun's
ribbons)
nastrini (tiny ribbons)

nodi Italiani
rags and tatters
ribbons and bows
sfrappole
striscie di vino
troubled thoughts
vanities
wands

Other names in other countries and cultures:

Chorage, csorage, hung chorage (Hungarian)
Fattigmand (Scandinavian)
fattigmanna Bakkels (Norwegian)
fattimanskor (Swedish)
filhozes (Portuguese)
krushki (Polish)
puzzles (Czechoslovakian)
twists (Scandinavian)
tayglach (Yiddish)

It's something that everybody tries to make, but nobody has the right recipe. So you put the dough together whatever way you know how, and they come out, and they're good anyway. —Grandma

Grandma's Favorite Gloves

6 eggs

1 cup sugar

$\frac{1}{2}$ teaspoon salt

$\frac{1}{2}$ cup melted shortening

$\frac{1}{2}$ cup olive oil

$\frac{1}{2}$ lemon, juice and grated rind

$\frac{1}{2}$ orange, juice and grated rind

$1\frac{1}{2}$ teaspoons lemon extract

$1\frac{1}{2}$ teaspoons anise extract

1 teaspoon vanilla

4 to 6 cups flour, more or less,
    depending on size of eggs

$1\frac{1}{2}$ tablespoons baking powder

oil for deep-frying

powdered sugar for dusting

1. Beat eggs. Add sugar, salt, shortening, and olive oil. Add flavorings to egg mixture.

2. Add 1 cup flour mixed with baking powder, then rest of flour.

3. Knead until soft but not sticky. Divide into 6 balls and let rest, covered.

4. Flatten each ball, one at a time, and roll into thin sheet. With fluted wheel, cut sheet into strips, 3 or 4 inches wide. Cut strips into diamonds.

5. Slit diamonds in middle. Pull one end of each diamond through slit.

6. Deep-fry and sprinkle with powdered sugar.

♦ *Makes* five or six dozen gloves

Note: See next page for more details.

How to Make Gloves

by Jody DeVivo

Anita started by cracking a few yolks, which we all laughed at. Then she melted the shortening and took this opportunity to show off her home economics training by teaching us the correct way to measure exactly one cup of shortening: You fill a measuring container with one cup of water, then you add the shortening until the water level is up to 2 cups.

She also explained that the best way to add the baking powder is to mix it in about a cup of the flour, and then add it to the rest. I guess it gets distributed more evenly that way. Boy, that Anita. She sure knows a thing or two.

Meanwhile, Judy was busy grating the orange rind, after a lengthy

Judy happily grates an orange peel at Grandma's in 1997.

These instructions are excerpted from *The Mama DeVivo Newsletter*, Issue 30, June 2, 1997. Grandma teaches Jody, Judy, and Anita how to make gloves.

discussion on which size of grater holes she should use. After grading the different grates, it was decided that the greatest grater holes weren't as great as the ones that were greater than the least. Understand? Great.

So . . . you put it all together, then you beat it all around and that's what we call uh . . . what do we call that anyway?

Anita actually forgot a very important step. She should have mixed all the ingredients with a spoon BEFORE using the electric mixer. That way flour doesn't go all over the place while it's still dry. Luckily, she remembered before it turned into a blizzard. Mixed it by hand for awhile. And then switched to the electric mixer.

"Here's how it's done. You take this thing and put it through there and then . . ."

Well, eventually it all turned into a nice ball of dough, which Anita divided into little balls of dough . . . with a little help from a friend (Grandma).

(If I had accidentally swallowed one of those little things you put in a man's shirt collar to keep it neat, and it made me cough out all over Anita while she was rolling the dough, would she have been considered a kneader in a stay hack?)

Now the little balls of dough needed to be rolled into thin flats of dough.

Now Comes the Fun Part

Using that crinkly wheel thingamajig, you cut the rolled-out dough into little strips. And then you make two vertical slits in each strip, one on top of the other.

Or you make more slits for even more fun. The rest is easy. . . .

After waiting patiently, Judy finally gets the gloves, one at a time, from Anita. She lowers each one into the simmering oil and watches a little glove ballet as the gnarled, tangled, dancing dough seems to sing out in its little cookie voice, "Ow-ow-ow! This is hot! Get me outta here!"

This is a critical point in the whole process. Because if you let them get as brown as you think they should look, you're overdoing it. They dry a bit darker than they look in the pot.

And the process goes on until all the little balls are rolled, stripped, slitted, tangled, and fried.

And last, the powdered sugar. This was my job when I wasn't taking pictures, and I must say, I did it very well.

Finalmente!

Bravo! Bravissimo! Bellissimo!
Also pretty nice.

Old-Fashioned Soft Pumpkin Cookies

I t's a good recipe. Mary [Grandma's friend] makes them. If they're done right, they're real delicate.   —Grandma

2 ½ cups all-purpose flour

1 teaspoon baking powder

1 teaspoon baking soda

½ teaspoon salt

1 teaspoon ground cinnamon

½ teaspoon ground nutmeg

½ cup butter or margarine, softened

1 ½ cups granulated sugar

1 cup solid pack pumpkin

1 egg

1 teaspoon vanilla

GLAZE

2 cups sifted powdered sugar

3 tablespoons milk

1 tablespoon melted butter or margarine

1 teaspoon vanilla extract

In medium bowl, combine flour, baking powder, baking soda, salt, cinnamon, and nutmeg. Set aside. In large mixer bowl, cream butter and sugar. Add pumpkin, egg, and vanilla; beat until light and creamy. Add dry ingredients; mix well. Drop by rounded tablespoons onto greased cookie sheets. Smooth tops of cookies. Bake in preheated 350-degree oven for 15 to 20 minutes, or until lightly browned. Cool on wire racks. Drizzle with glaze.

Glaze: In small bowl, combine powdered sugar, milk, melted butter, and vanilla extract. Blend until smooth.

Stir into batter any one of the following:

1 cup raisins

1 cup chopped nuts

1 cup uncooked rolled oats and ½ cup pineapple, drained

1 cup raisins and 1 cup chopped nuts

◆ *Makes* three dozen cookies

Peggy Pogue's Sugar Cookies

When Gram moved to Wilmette, Beck and I would go over to her townhouse each year and help her make these sugar cookies. Sometimes we'd make nontraditional-shaped cookies of our own creation (such as the boy I had a crush on in sixth grade), which she laughed at but always made us eat immediately.   —Kate

1 stick butter

1 cup sugar

1 egg

1 teaspoon vanilla

1¾ cups flour

2 teaspoons baking powder

¼ teaspoon salt

Additional sugar

Food coloring

Cream butter and sugar. Beat in egg; add vanilla. Add flour, baking powder, and salt.

Roll thin and cut with cookie cutters. Bake 12 minutes at 350 degrees.

Mix sugar, about ⅛ cup, with a couple drops of food coloring. Stir well. Sprinkle colored sugar over tops of cookies when done.

◆ *Makes* about four dozen average-sized sugar cookies

Grandma's Favorite Pizzelles

Sometimes called waffles, brigidini, cialdi, or ferratelle.

2 sticks margarine

1½ cups sugar

6 eggs

2 teaspoons vanilla

¾ teaspoon anise oil

3½ to 4 cups flour

2 teaspoons baking powder

Melt margarine. Blend with sugar. Add eggs and flavorings. Mix flour and baking powder and add to batter. Drop on pizzelle iron* by teaspoonfuls.

◆ *Makes* sixty or more regular sized cookies or seventy-five to one hundred small ones, depending on how small they are.

A pizzelle iron can be bought at any department store or cooking store, or on eBay.

Joe and Jody's Pizzelles

(LOOSELY BASED ON GRANDMA'S RECIPE)

In our house, the making of waffle cookies has been taken over by Jody and Joey. This is how they do it.   —Judy

1 pound shortening	3 tablespoons anise
3 cups sugar	4 teaspoons baking powder
12 eggs	3 tablespoons vanilla
Pinch salt	9 to 12 cups flour

Melt shortening. In bowl, mix with sugar. Beat in eggs. Add salt, anise, baking powder, and vanilla. Stir in flour. Roll into walnut-size balls and cook in pizzelle iron.

◆ *Makes* six to eight dozen pizzelles

They'll get it right one of these days! —Evelyn

JOEY'S 1991 ALTERATIONS

1. Use 9 cups plus 3 handfuls of self-rising flour.
2. Do not use salt or baking powder.
3. Use 1½ tablespoons of anise. And then make sure you add 1 shot of very old sambuca.

After hours of work . . . the Christmas plate is ready to go.

Judy's Chocolate Balls

This recipe comes from my mother, Peggy, although she never actually made them. She ate some at a party in Washington, D.C., once, loved them, asked for the recipe, then handed it to me and said, "Here, these are delicious!" (They really are, but very rich!) Greta (friend and editor of the first version of this book) says her family calls them "Buckeyes."   —Judy

2 sticks margarine
2 cups graham cracker crumbs
1 12-ounce jar peanut butter
1 cup coconut (optional)
1 cup ground nuts
1 pound powdered sugar
1 teaspoon vanilla

½ cake paraffin (available in canning section of grocery stores)
1 12-ounce package chocolate chips
1 square unsweetened chocolate (or use an additional 12-ounce package chocolate chips)

Melt margarine. Add graham cracker crumbs, peanut butter, coconut, nuts, powdered sugar, and vanilla. Stir and mix well. Make into small balls and let dry overnight.

In a double boiler, melt paraffin, chocolate chips, and unsweetened chocolate. Keep mixture in double boiler to keep heated, and dip balls in the mixture. Dry on wax paper.

♦ *Makes* three to four dozen

Anita's Anise Biscotti

4½ cups all-purpose flour

1 teaspoon baking powder

1 teaspoon baking soda

1 teaspoon salt

2 large eggs

1 cup sugar

¾ cup vegetable oil

½ cup sour cream

1 teaspoon vanilla

½ teaspoon anise seeds (optional)

2 teaspoons anise extract or

    ¾ teaspoon anise oil

½ cup chopped walnuts (optional)

½ cup raisins

Egg wash: egg yolk and

    1 teaspoon water beaten

    together

Preheat oven to 350 degrees and lightly oil a large baking sheet. In one bowl, whisk together flour, baking powder, baking soda, and salt. In another bowl, beat together eggs, sugar, and vegetable oil until well combined. Beat in sour cream, vanilla, and anise flavorings. Add flour mixture gradually, beating until mixture forms a dough. Stir in walnuts and raisins.

Turn dough out onto a lightly floured surface and divide into three pieces. Form each piece into a log about 14 inches long and 2 inches wide and arrange a few inches apart on baking sheet. Brush logs with egg wash and bake in middle of oven 30 minutes, or until pale golden brown. Cool logs on baking sheet 10 minutes and carefully transfer to a cutting board.

Cut each log diagonally into 1-inch thick slices and cool on racks, or bake another 15 minutes for crunchy biscotti. Keep in airtight containers for one week, or frozen, one month.

• *Makes* about forty-eight biscotti

Grandma's Wedding Cookies

6 eggs

¾ cup oil

1 cup or less of sugar

1 tablespoon anise or
   2 tablespoons lemon
   extract

1 teaspoon vanilla

Pinch salt

3 tablespoons baking powder

4½ cups flour

ICING

2 tablespoons margarine

4 tablespoons milk

2 cups powdered sugar

Food coloring

In large bowl mix first six ingredients at high speed for 5 to 10 minutes. Mix the baking powder with 1 cup of the flour and add. Then gradually add remaining flour as needed, the less the better. Mix by hand. Work dough until it feels right. Let it sit.

To form cookies, make little balls or circles. Bake for 7 to 8 minutes at 375 degrees, or, for a more delicate color, a little longer at 325 degrees. Cool before icing.

♦ *Makes* five to six dozen cookies

Note: These cookies are usually iced in pastel colors.

Grandma's Te-Tus

This is a small batch of the recipe Grandma made for Janice's wedding. The wedding recipe used 3 pounds of flour, making 200 cookies per recipe, and was made several times. Grandma insisted that the Te-Tus be iced by turning them in a bowl so the icing wouldn't be too smooth. Several of her grandchildren learned to make these cookies, and they often sent her some in a care package. Grandma always thought they were too big but she had to admit they were tasty.   —Anita

1 cup margarine plus ¼ cup oil

1¼ cups sugar

2 eggs

1 cup milk

1 orange, juice and grated rind

1 lemon, juice and grated rind

2 tablespoons vanilla

½ cup cocoa

1 cup plus 3½ to 5 or 6 cups flour

1 teaspoon baking soda

2 tablespoons baking powder

1 3- or 4-ounce package peanuts,
    coarsely ground

Preheat oven to 350 degrees. Prepare cookie sheets. Cream margarine, oil, and sugar; beat in eggs. Add milk, orange juice and rind, lemon juice and rind, and vanilla. Combine cocoa, 1 cup flour, baking soda, and baking powder. Add to mixture. Gradually add remaining flour to make tender dough. Add peanuts. To shape cookies, roll long ropes about ½-inch thick, cut pieces about 2 inches long, and arrange on cookie sheets. Bake for 10 to 12 minutes. Cool. Ice with powdered sugar icing (see page 196). Pour icing into big bowl, add cookies, and stir with your hands to coat. Let dry.

◆ *Makes* three or four dozen cookies

Peggy's Nutty Fingers

⅔ cup butter

4 tablespoons powdered sugar

1 tablespoon ice water

2 cups cake flour

1 teaspoon vanilla

1 cup ground pecans

Powdered sugar to roll
    cookies in

Cream butter and powdered sugar. Add water, flour, and vanilla. Fold in nuts. Roll into finger shapes. Bake at 350 degrees for 25 minutes. Roll in powdered sugar while hot.

• *Makes* two dozen cookies

Debbie and Kenny watch as Kate and Beck strive for the perfectly art-directed cookie tray (a very important job) for desert on Christmas Eve.

The Chocolate Chip Cookie Contest

by Kate DeVivo et al.

Way back in the early '90s, a discussion dominated Christmas Eve dinner at the DeVivo house in Chicago. There were so many chocolate chip cookies. Kate and Kenny made a batch each; Peg made her traditional Nestle Tollhouses; Uncle Bill added some to the crowd; and Joe showed up with Mint Chocolate Chip cookies. Some had nuts; some were flat; some were exceptionally chewy; others were just okay. The question arose: "What makes a chocolate chip cookie stand above the rest?" The following year, Jody elected himself Chocolate Chip Cookie Chairman and sent the following rules to the family. —Kate

In Search of the Perfect Chocolate Chip Cookie: A Brief History

by Jody DeVivo

For centuries, every Chocolate Chip Cookie, while ultimately judged in the mouth of the beholder, nevertheless had to meet certain traditional and immutable criteria before it

could be considered a "player" in man's and woman's never-ending quest for the Perfect Chocolate Chip Cookie. However, in recent years certain upstarts, who shall remain nameless, have politicked to have various variations, innovations, and mutations of the Basic Chocolate Chip Cookie share the same tables and palates with the original. While conservative "Chippers" fought valiantly to protect the purity of their cookie, these Young Turks (or Tongue Jerks as one of the old guard called them) made such a fuss and whined so much that a whole new category of Chocolate Chip Cookies was recognized by the International Cookie Congress—The Bastard Chip Cookie. In addition, to protect the integrity of the Basics and promote quality among the Bastards, the ICC also released the following set of rules by which every Chocolate Chip, whether Basic or Bastard, should be judged.

THE CHOCOLATE CHIP STANDARD

1. The ideal Chocolate Chip Cookie must not have too few chips.

Non Basta, Cheapaskate!

2. The ideal Chocolate Chip Cookie must not have too many chips.

Tutti Grosso al' Acne.

3. The ideal Chocolate Chip Cookie contains a number of chips that are exactly just right.

Perfecto, Molto Bene, Justa Right.

4. Dunkability is important—the cookie must not shed coffee or milk like a London Fog.

5. However, when the cookie is full of coffee, milk, or on some occasions wine, it must not break under the added weight, making an ungodly mess and embarrassing the dunker.

6. The ideal Chocolate Chip Cookie has a texture that doesn't get brittle until three days after baking, or seven, if left in an unopened cookie tin.

7. The ideal Chocolate Chip Cookie is not crumby.

8. If the cookie contains nuts, the nuts must never dominate.

9. The thickness of the cookie should never exceed the height of two chocolate chips.

10. The shape should be roundish as opposed to squarish or rectangularish.

11. The size should never be more than a hungry person can put into his mouth without breaking it apart, nor should it be small enough to fit two in at a single time and still be able to smile.

12. The mountains on the cookie's surface should never exceed a chocolate chip's height above the valleys'.

13. The rest is a matter of taste.

(Note: During all international competitions, these are the rules used to determine the Best Basic Chip Cookie, the Best Bastard Chip Cookie, and a Best of Show Chip.)

Despite Jody's self-election as Chocolate Chip Cookie Chairman, it was decided a few years later that whoever won the contest would then make the rules for the following year. And since its establishment, the International Cookie Congress has certainly changed some of the rules and regulations:

"The ICC has recently nominated me *(Beck)* as the new chairman. As a result, I have taken it upon myself to change all the rules that I think were silly, useless, or more importantly, Chippist. I am sorry to admit that, in the past, we have discriminated against cookies that were too 'white' or too 'cinnamon.' Granted, some of them really were bad cookies. Nevertheless, this year there will be no separate categories. There will be no 'bastard' chip cookie. All cookies will be admitted and voted on. However, if you want to win, it is important to consider the fact that there may still be Chippist judges."

Carl's Chocolate Chips

Cousin Rose once complained to Grandma that she got too few cookies with her chocolate chip recipe. Grandma disappeared into the cellar and returned with a trash bag full of chocolate chip cookies. She plopped it on the kitchen table and said, "You have to adjust recipes—add flour— think 'four boys.'"

1⅓ cup shortening (part butter
   or margarine)

1 cup sugar

1 cup brown sugar (firmly packed)

2 eggs

2 teaspoons vanilla

3 cups flour

1 teaspoon baking soda

1 teaspoon salt

1 cup chopped nuts (optional)

1 12-ounce package chocolate
   chips

Heat oven to 375 degrees. Mix shortening, sugars, eggs, and vanilla thoroughly. Mix flour, baking soda, and salt separately. Mix dry ingredients with wet ingredients. Add nuts and chocolate chips. Drop by rounded tablespoons on ungreased cookie sheet. Bake for 10 to 13 minutes.

• *Makes* four or five dozen cookies

Grandma's Blueberry Bars

1 ½ cups shortening

1 ¼ cups sugar

6 eggs

1 ½ cups milk

1 teaspoon anise oil

6 teaspoons baking powder

6 cups flour

1 21-ounce can blueberry
    pie filling

Any white icing (see pages 196,
    214)

1. Cream shortening and sugar. Add eggs, milk, and anise oil. Add baking powder and flour.

2. Turn dough out and shape into two long loaves (as long as a standard cookie sheet). Roll each loaf out into a rectangle. Spoon blueberries down the center of each rectangle. Fold long edges over to cover filling, then short edges to close. Scratch over the seams with a fork to seal.

3. Bake until golden brown. Remove and cool before icing. To serve, cut into slices.

♦ *Makes* about two dozen cookies

Stella's Peanut Butter Squares

1 box yellow cake mix

1 stick plus 2 tablespoons
   margarine, divided

1 cup peanut butter

2 eggs

1 12-ounce package of chocolate
   chips

1 14-ounce can condensed milk

1. Set oven to 350 degrees and grease 9 × 13-inch pan.

2. Mix together cake mix, 1 stick margarine, peanut butter, and eggs.

3. Divide mixture in half. Pat one-half in bottom of greased pan.

4. Melt chocolate chips (in double boiler or saucepan, or in microwave).
Add 2 tablespoons margarine and milk.

5. Spread mixture over layer in the pan and spread other half of cake
mixture over it.

6. Bake for 20 minutes.

7. Cool and cut into squares.

♦ *Makes* about four dozen cookies

This recipe is from Stella DeVivo, cousin Alphonso's wife.   —*Anita*

Zuppa Inglese

As a teenager, my role model was my mother's youngest sister, Stella. On one occasion she returned to New Castle from New York with a recipe for a dessert she had tasted in the big city. Once I tasted it, it became one of my "keepers." Mom always made it from scratch, but that was before instant vanilla pudding was available. We have all shortened it one way or another, the new products are quicker and almost as delicious.   —Evelyn

1 package instant French vanilla
   pudding
8-ounce jar maraschino cherries,
   halved and drained

1 sponge cake, ring style
Crème de cacao, up to $\frac{1}{2}$ cup
Whiskey or rum, up to $\frac{1}{2}$ cup
Whipped cream, 1 cup or more

Make pudding according to directions on box. Mix cherries into pudding.

This dessert is layered as follows. First layer: narrowly sliced sponge cake to cover bottom of 8 × 10 serving dish. Liberally sprinkle crème de cacao and whiskey/rum over cake layer. Spread pudding mixture over all. Repeat for second layer. Top with third layer of sponge cake and cover with whipped cream.

◆ *Serves* six

Rox's Rockin' Cheesecake

You want a recipe? Here's a good one. This one has gotten me more marriage proposals from men AND women than I know what to do with (obviously, since I've not accepted one of them yet). For some reason, even people who don't know me ask me to make them cheesecake.

—Roxanne

2 8-ounce packages of cream
   cheese
1 cup sugar plus ½ cup, divided
1 smallish container (1 cup) of
   whipped cottage cheese
5 eggs

A few teaspoons of vanilla
2 premade graham cracker crusts
   (believe me, they'll never
   know)
1 medium container of sour cream

Filling

Cream together the cream cheese with 1 cup sugar and about a heaping cup of cottage cheese. Add the eggs one at a time. Add (ohmygawd, they have the CUTEST white Bengal tiger cubs on the *Today Show*—they're as big as their mom's foot, awwww) . . . anyway, add a few teaspoons of vanilla (I never measure this stuff), pour it into the two crusts, bake for about an hour or so at around 325 degrees. Check by sticking a knife in the center, blah blah blah.

Icing

Now, what I like to do for the icing is mix the container of sour cream with about ½ cup of sugar and around a teaspoon of vanilla. Then, ice the cakes while they're hot and let them cool. When they're cool, invert the little plastic thingies the crusts came with and—Bam! You've got covered cheesecakes that stack beautifully in your agonizingly small apartment refrigerator.

I usually bake about one day before an event so they can settle. Serve with fruit, sit back and let the accolades roll, sister!

◆ *Makes* two pies

Debbie's Apple Walnut Bundt Cake

3 cups all-purpose flour
1¾ cups sugar
1 teaspoon baking soda
1 teaspoon ground cinnamon
¾ teaspoon salt
¼ teaspoon ground nutmeg
1 cup vegetable oil
½ cup apple juice

2 teaspoons vanilla
3 large eggs
3 medium-size Golden Delicious
   or Granny Smith apples, peeled,
   cored, and coarsely chopped
1 cup coarsely chopped walnuts
1 cup golden raisins
Powdered sugar for dusting

1. Preheat oven to 350 degrees.

2. Measure all ingredients into large bowl except apples, walnuts, raisins, and powdered sugar. With the mixer at low speed, beat until mixed, scraping sides of bowl. Increase speed to medium; beat 2 minutes, occasionally scraping bowl. Stir in apples, walnuts, and raisins.

3. Spoon batter into Bundt pan, spreading evenly. Bake for 1 hour 15 minutes, or until cake pulls away from pan. Cool cake for 10 minutes.

4. Invert cake; remove from pan and cool completely.

5. Sprinkle with powdered sugar before serving.

♦ *Serves* sixteen

G.G.'s Baked Custard

3 eggs

½ cup sugar

¼ teaspoon salt

1 pint milk, heated

½ teaspoon vanilla

Nutmeg to taste

Beat eggs. Add sugar and salt. Add heated milk. Add vanilla and nutmeg. Pour into baking dish and bake at 375 degrees for 45 minutes.

♦ *Serves* four to six

Anita's Lemon Ice

4 cups water

1½ cups sugar

Juice of 6 lemons (strained) *or*

    12 tablespoons bottled juice *or*

    1 bottle frozen juice, adjusting

    water to 5⅓ cups and

    increasing sugar to 2¼ cups

1 egg white

Additional ¼ cup sugar

Heat water and 1½ cups sugar until sugar is melted, about 2 to 3 minutes. Add lemon juice. Cool. Pour into ice tray and freeze until mushy. Do not let it solidify. Scrape sides of tray and pour into a chilled bowl. Stir until smooth but not melted.

Beat egg white until frothy. Add ¼ cup sugar until the egg white forms peaks. Stir the egg white into the lemon mixture. Freeze until firm, stirring from time to time to even out the texture.

♦ *Makes* one-half gallon; serves six

Judy's Citrus Trifle

2 large lemons

1 large orange

2 8-ounce packages cream cheese,
   softened

2 cups powdered sugar

2 teaspoons lemon extract

1 ½ pints heavy or whipping cream

2 3-ounce packages ladyfingers

Strawberries for garnish

1. Squeeze juice from lemons. Reserve. Grate, peel, and squeeze juice from orange. Reserve 1 teaspoon grated orange peel for garnish.

2. In large bowl, with mixer at low speed, beat cream cheese, powdered sugar, lemon extract, reserved lemon juice, and remaining grated orange peel until blended.

3. In another large bowl, with mixer at medium speed, beat cream until stiff peaks form. With rubber spatula, fold whipped cream into cream cheese mixture.

4. Split each ladyfinger. Brush flat side with orange juice. Line bottom and side of a 3-quart glass soufflé dish or trifle bowl, with the rounded side of ladyfingers against the dish.

5. Spoon filling into the dish. Arrange strawberries on top, sprinkle with grated orange peel.

6. Refrigerate at least 2 hours.

• *Serves* **twelve**

Note: This has become another part of our Christmas feast. —*Judy*

Babs's Peach Dessert

1 16-ounce can sliced peaches

½ to 1 cup brown sugar

1 butter cake mix

1 stick butter or margarine

Pour can of peaches (juice and all) into greased casserole. Sprinkle with brown sugar. Pour dry cake mix evenly over peaches and dot with butter. Bake at 350 degrees for 30 to 35 minutes, or until tested with toothpick and it comes out clean.

AUNT JANE'S VARIATION

Line a baking pan with graham crackers and pour in 1 28- to 30-ounce can cherries (cherry pie filling) or peaches and 1 cup chopped walnuts. Sift 1 package white cake mix over filling and spread around pan. Pour ¼ cup melted butter over top. Bake at 300 degrees for 1 hour.

• *Serves* six to eight

Note: Some people may prefer to sprinkle smaller amounts of brown sugar. It depends on individual taste, though peaches should be well covered with the sugar.

Aunt's Easter Bread

DOUGH

1 dozen eggs

4 cups sugar

½ pound lard

¼ pound butter

2 cakes yeast

1 tablespoon salt

3 cups water

5 pounds flour

1 1-ounce bottle anise extract

1 1-ounce bottle lemon extract

ICING

2 cups powdered sugar

1 egg

¼ cup margarine

1 teaspoon lemon extract

Milk, as needed to make icing
    smooth

Shelley's first loaf of Easter bread
—lessons from Evelyn at Judy and
Jody's.

After making dough,* let rise once, knock down.
Get pans ready. Divide into equal portions and
shape loaves. Bake at 250 degrees to 275 degrees
for 30 to 40 minutes.

♦ *Makes* about eight to ten loaves

*In Zia (Aunt) Gaetana DeMasi's time, and Grand-
ma's, everybody knew how to make bread, so there
was no need for instructions. Grandma probably
copied these instructions down by watching Gaetana,
who was called "Aunt," work. The recipe is dated
1960, when Aunt was in her late 70s. A year later,
Grandma wrote, "Recipe good, not too sweet. Tried
same dough for bunny heads and nut rolls with honey
(good). Have all ingredients at room temperature.
Put in stove to raise with pan of hot water to cut
raising time. Made in morning."*

Grandma's Easter Rice

Grandma usually made four or five big pans of Easter Rice at once, and we often ate it cooled. As the years passed and times were easier, Grandma would bake the rice without the crust as a treat on days other than Easter.   —Anita

1 pound rice

1 ½ cups sugar

½ teaspoon salt

½ cup margarine

4 ounces citron (optional)

1 to 2 ounces lemon flavoring

1 dozen eggs, beaten

1 quart milk

½ to 1 cup raisins (optional)

Dabs of butter or margarine

Preheat oven to 375 degrees. Cook rice according to package directions. Add sugar, salt, margarine, citron, if using, and lemon flavoring and stir to melt margarine and sugar. When rice is cool, add beaten eggs, milk, and, if using, raisins. Grease and flour baking pans or line with crust (see accompanying recipe). Pour rice into the pans and scatter dabs of butter or margarine on top. Bake until firm and lightly browned.

Grandma's Crust for Easter Rice

6 tablespoons vegetable oil or
    ½ cup shortening

¼ cup sugar

3 eggs

1 cup milk (optional)

1 teaspoon vanilla

2 cups or more flour

2 teaspoons baking powder

¼ teaspoon salt

In one bowl, blend oil or shortening and sugar. Add eggs, milk, and vanilla. Mix flour, baking powder, and salt in separate bowl and add to eggs. Work dough and divide into two pieces. Roll out and fit into baking pans, leaving some extra dough hanging over edges. Pour rice into pans, drawing extra dough up over rice as far as it will go to make a border. If there is enough dough, cut strips and make lattice on top.

◆ *Serves* two to three dozen

THE LAMB CAKE

Grandma once wrote in to a radio show after hearing a program about Easter Lamb Cakes. This is what she wrote, in 1992:

I am an old timer of 86 years listening to this program today. I'm surprised how little is known of the Easter Lamb Cake. It was in the 1930s we bought a lamb mold for $1.98. We were three neighbors living in a row of houses, and we were interested in making lambs for our children.

My sister went to Pittsburgh and bought one at Gimbel's or Kaufman's. We all went to work and made one. There was no recipe with the mold. We had to improvise and tried all sorts of recipes.

Soon we got good with them. We made them for neighbors, for church doings, our mothers' friends, etc. Pretty soon they were being made by pastry shops, etc. Eventually we got tired. The lambs were so popular the novelty wore off. I was left with the mold and nobody claimed it. I finally passed it on to my children who lived out of town, and that's where it is.

To make a good lamb, do not make a very tender cake, no nuts or raisins, a plain cake. Keep the mold clean and flour it after greasing.

Before putting the lamb in the oven, put one lollipop stick across the forehead and one in the middle of the neck so it will never break off. Use raisins for eyes and half or quarter of a candied cherry for lips. Use icing and coconut for fur. And tie a ribbon around the neck.

When I asked Grandma about the Lamb Cake, here's what she said. —Kate

When I first got married in the mid-1920s, all the ladies were making Easter bread. Aunt Lizzie and I had lambs. We were the first in Mahoningtown to make them! At first they were a novelty, and we would make them for everyone and everything. We were so proud. We became quite popular at that time . . . everybody became curious about the lamb. "Where'd you get the lamb?" they'd ask. Pretty soon, though, everyone had them and made them. By then, we were done with them.

Debbie's Fool's Toffee

Saltine crackers
(approximately 40)
2 sticks butter (no substitutes)
1 cup dark brown sugar

1 12-ounce package milk chocolate
chips
½ to 1 cup chopped pecans or
walnuts

Line bottom and sides of cookie sheet with foil and grease lightly with butter. Place crackers on bottom of foil so they fit close together (you may have to carefully break some of the crackers to fit in pan).

In a medium saucepan, melt butter along with brown sugar and boil for 4 minutes. (IMPORTANT!)

Pour over crackers, spreading to make sure crackers are covered. Bake in 370-degree oven for 5 minutes. Melt chocolate in a double boiler or microwave. Take crackers out of oven and immediately spread chocolate over this.

After spreading chocolate, sprinkle with nuts. Pat lightly so they adhere to the chocolate. Cool at room temperature and refrigerate for several hours or overnight. Peel foil from bottom and break toffee into serving pieces.

◆ *Makes* twenty-four

Babs's Fudge

1 cup sugar

1 cup milk

½ cup water

½ teaspoon salt

2 squares unsweetened chocolate

2 tablespoons white corn syrup

2 tablespoons butter

½ teaspoon vanilla

Combine sugar, milk, water, salt, chocolate, and corn syrup in pan over low heat. Stir till sugar dissolves. Take a little bit of chocolate and drop into cold water. If it forms a ball, then it's done.

Remove from heat. Drop in butter. Don't stir! Set aside to cool.

Add vanilla and beat with mixer on medium speed till it loses gloss and holds shape. Turn onto greased 9 × 13 pan. Cool and cut into squares.

◆ *Makes* three dozen

Breakfast

- Grandma's Frittata
- Debbie's Breakfast Pizza
- Judy's Apple Cheddar Soufflé
- Katie's Dutch Puff
- Jody's Mother's Day Brunch
- Roxanne's Morning Wake-up Call
- Joe's Hangover Potatoes

Grandma's Frittata

1 large onion, chopped

1 to 2 tablespoons good olive oil

2 sliced zucchini or a small bunch
of asparagus cut into 2-inch
strips

5 eggs

¼ cup Parmesan or Romano
cheese

Salt and pepper to taste

Start sautéing onion in oil. Add zucchini or asparagus. While they are cooking, beat eggs with Parmesan or Romano cheese, salt and pepper. When
vegetables are tender, stir in eggs and let cook until top begins to dry.

At this point, cook with a lid on, until eggs are firm, or put pan into oven or
try to turn frittata over to finish cooking eggs. To turn over, cut into quar-
ters and turn each quarter with a big spatula.

• *Serves* four

*Kate, Anita and Grandma used
zucchini cut into half-moons. Yum.*

Debbie's Breakfast Pizza

1 pound pork sausage
1 cup frozen hash browns, thawed
1 cup shredded sharp Cheddar
   cheese

5 large eggs
¼ cup milk
⅛ teaspoon pepper
2 tablespoons Parmesan cheese

Brown sausage, drain, and put in 10-inch pie plate. Cover with hash browns, then sprinkle with Cheddar cheese. Beat eggs, milk, and pepper together. Pour over Cheddar cheese. Sprinkle with Parmesan.

Bake 30 to 35 minutes at 375 degrees, until slightly puffed and knife inserted in center comes out clean.

If made ahead, refrigerate. To reheat, cover with aluminum foil and bake at 350 degrees for 20 to 30 minutes.

♦ *Serves* four to six

Judy's Apple Cheddar Soufflé

I make this ahead of time for Christmas morning or other holidays, so I don't have to worry about it. It's really easy to make ahead of time and just throw in the oven when you have company!   —Judy

4 slices white bread, cubed

1 12-ounce package frozen
    scalloped apples, thawed

1 cup chopped cooked ham

¾ cup shredded sharp Cheddar
    cheese

4 eggs

¼ cup half-and-half

Pepper to taste

1. Spray 9-inch deep-dish pie pan with cooking spray. Arrange bread cubes in bottom of sprayed pan. Spoon apples evenly over bread; sprinkle evenly with ham and cheese.

2. In medium bowl, combine eggs, half-and-half, and pepper; mix well. Carefully pour over apples, ham, and cheese. Cover with plastic wrap; refrigerate at least 6 hours, or overnight.

3. Heat oven to 350 degrees. Bake uncovered for 40 to 45 minutes, or until top is lightly browned and center is set. Let stand 10 to 15 minutes before serving.

◆ *Serves* six

Katie's Dutch Puff

This is the first recipe I ever learned to make. My family loved it—particularly my mom, because I would kick everyone out of the kitchen except my sister, who I tried to make help me (she sometimes did, reluctantly).   —Kate

1 cup flour
1 cup milk
4 eggs
¾ cup butter or margarine

Preheat oven to 425 degrees. Mix together flour, milk, and eggs to the consistency of pancake batter. In a deep baking dish or casserole, melt butter. Pour batter into casserole and bake for about 20 minutes. (Batter should have risen above rim of casserole and lightly browned.) Serve with maple syrup.

♦ *Serves* four to six

JODY'S MOTHER'S DAY BRUNCH

1 to 2 pounds fresh jumbo shrimp

Shrimp sauce

1 thing of tuna salad from the deli counter

1 thing of cole slaw from the deli counter

Bloody Marys

English muffins, toasted

Blintzes that the grocery store woman
    convinces you are FANTASTIC

Blintz sauce

Go to local grocery store. Buy above items. Serve in real
dishes.

◆ *Servings* vary

ROXANNE'S MORNING WAKE-UP CALL

by Roxanne Aubrey

I think some of my boyfriends stayed with me a little longer than they should have, because my coffee is so good.

First, and most important, you MUST buy good, dark coffee beans. Don't scrimp. And get yourself a grinder, for Pete's sake. (I recommend the cordless grinder because the cords on the other grinders tend to curl up with frequent use, which is VERY irritating first thing in the morning.)

Next, get one of those single stove-top espresso pots. And never wash it with soap and water. That is a sin. Just rinse it off.

So fill the bottom part of the pot with water up to the little vent hole, put the coffee holder in it, and fill the coffee holder up to the very top. None of this two-teaspoon-only crap. To the top. No air, only coffee. Screw on the top and wait for the beautiful gurgling sound.

While that's brewing, nuke about a cup of milk. Whole milk, skim is for wimps. Make sure to scald it good.

When the coffee is done, pour it and the scalded milk into a big cup. Add sugar if you must. The zotz of the caffeine negates the need for any more throughout the day. Trust me.

Oh, and this coffee tastes best when you eat something sweet with it.

Joe's Hangover Potatoes

2 potatoes—the bigger, the better

1 onion—white, not yellow

A bunch of mushrooms

1 to 2 tablespoons olive oil, plus
more as needed

At least 2 cloves of garlic, minced,
chopped, or crushed

Any spices on hand: oregano, basil,
rosemary, thyme, pepper, and
Italian seasoning to taste

Creole seasoning to taste

1. Slice potatoes thinly.

2. Chop onion.

3. Slice mushrooms.

4. Heat up oil in large frying pan and add potatoes.

5. After potatoes have gotten a head start, add onions and garlic.

6. When onions "limpen" (as Aunt Evelyn likes to say), add spices, and lots of 'em. Careful with the Creole seasoning, though. It's a salt substitute, and it has a kick to it.

7. Add mushrooms.

8. When potatoes are golden brown and taste good, they're done.

• *Serves* two to four, depending on how hungover you and others are

INDEX

beer (porter; stout): in chili, 45
  in skippers, 23
biscotti, anise, 195
biscuit mix, for zucchini casse-
    role, 160
blueberry bars (cookies), 204
bone, meat, in soup, 43, 44
bouillon cubes, 43
braciole, 95–96
bread: for asparagus rolls, 20
  for bruschetta, 8
  Easter, 214
  fried (pizza fritte), 155
  frozen dough, for pizza crust,
    59
  in malfatti, 131
  quick dough for, 7
  in soufflé, 225
bread crumbs: for baked fish,
    109
  in braciole, 95
  in crab cakes, 17
  in malfatti, 131
  in meatballs, 30, 63
  in meatloaf, 94
  in stuffed artichokes, 113
  in stuffed peppers, 102
brigidini. See pizzelles
brine, for pickled eggplant, 161
broccoli-corn bake, 150
broth (stock): beef, in soup, 39
  chicken, 29
    in pilaf, 122
    in risotto, 107
    in soup, 40, 42
  vegetable, in pilaf, 122
bruschetta, tomato, 8
bulgur wheat, and lentil pilaf,
    122

cabbage: and beans, 123, 146
  in minestrone, 43

cake: apple walnut Bundt, 209
  lamb, 217
  sponge (premade), for zuppa
    inglese, 206
cake mix: in cookies, 205
  in fruit desserts, 213
candy: fool's toffee, 219
  fudge, 220
cantaloupe, in fruit slaw, 178
carrots: canned, for Swiss steak,
    98
  in fruit slaw, 178
  marinated, 143
  mustard, 144
  in pasta salad, 171
  with pilaf, 122
  in soup, 43
celery: and apple salad, 168
  in bean salad, 169
  in chicken salad, 174
  and olive relish, 15
  in pasta salad, 171
  seasoned (pinzimonio), 16
  in soup, 44
cheese: American, in macaroni
    and cheese, 152
  in pasta salad, 171
  for antipasto, 14
  Asiago, for antipasto, 14
  in manicotti, 62
  blue, in asparagus rolls, 20
  Cheddar, and apple soufflé,
    225
  in dip, 6
  in onion pie, 156
  on pizza, 224
  in quesadillas, 129
  cottage, in cheesecake, 207
  cream, in asparagus rolls, 20
  in cheesecake, 207
  in citrus trifle, 212
  and olive dip, 6

and pepper jelly appetizer, 10
  and pineapple salad, 166
  on pizza, 61
  and shrimp appetizer, 10
  feta, in salad, 170, 172
  goat, in salad, 163
  Gorgonzola, for antipasto, 14
  mozzarella, for antipasto, 14
  packaged shredded, in quesa-
    dillas, 129
  Parmesan, with baked
    chicken, 85
  in braciole, 95
  in dip, 5
  in eggplant parmigiana, 117
  in malfatti, 131
  in meatballs, 30
  with polenta, 127, 128
  for soup, 42
  provolone, for antipasto, 14
  ricotta, in manicotti, 62
  on pizza, 61
  in polenta lasagna, 128
  Romano, in braciole, 95
  in pasta salad, 171
  on pizza, 61
  in stuffing, 102, 113
  sheep milk, in salad, 170
  and tomato pizza, 49–51
cheesecake, 207–8
cherries, and cake mix dessert,
    213
  maraschino, 166, 206
chicken: breasts, baked with
    cheese, 85
  oriental salad of, 177
  stir-fried, 90–91
  broth, 29
  cacciatore, 89
  pieces, baked, with rosemary,
    83
  with sour cream, 84

salad, hot, 174
oriental, 177
stir-fried, with pineapple, 90–91
wings, deep-fried, 12
chile. *See* peppers
chili: beef, 105
venison, 45
chocolate: balls (cookies), 194
bits, 205
chip cookies, 203
about, 199–202
chips, 194, 203, 219
fudge, 220
cialdi. *See* pizzelles
cioppino, 40
citron, 215
coating: for baked chicken, 84
for deep-fried smelts, 18
coconut, in chocolate cookies, 194
coffee, 228–29
cole slaw, packaged, 164, 177
coogootz, 118
with sausage, 119
cookies: blueberry bars, 204
chocolate balls, 194
chocolate chip, 203
about, 199–202
gloves, 185–88
nutty finger, 198
peanut butter squares, 205
pumpkin, 188–90
sugar, 191
Te-Tus, 197
wedding, 196
see also biscotti; pizzelles
corn: canned, cream-style, with broccoli, 150
and pasta, 71
in Spanish rice, 130
in macaroni and cheese, 152

in stuffed peppers, 102
in succotash, 41
cornmeal, for polenta, 125, 127
cream: in pasta sauce, 80
whipped, 166, 208, 212
see also sour cream
croutons, 39
cucumber: in salad, 170
in soup, 34
with sour cream, 165
curry powder, in soup, 35

desserts: cheesecake, 207–8
cherry, 213
citrus trifle, 212
custard, baked, 210
Easter rice, 215–16
lemon ice, 211
peach, 213
zuppa inglese, 206
see also cake
dip: artichoke, 5
cream cheese and olive, 6
dough: for Easter bread, 214
pasta, 76–78
pizza, 49–50
quick bread, 155
dressing: for bean salad, 169
for codfish salad, 175
for fruit slaw, 178
for pasta salad, 173
drinks: margarita, 22
martini, 25
sangria, 21
vodka, and beer (skippers), 23
and lemonade, 24
Dutch puff, 226

eggplant: in moussaka, 137
parmigiana, 117
pickled, 161–62
in stuffed manicotti, 62

eggs: for antipasto, 14
apple and Cheddar cheese soufflé, 225
baked custard, 210
in béchamel sauce, 137
on breakfast pizza, 224
creamed, on toast, 135
deviled, 7
in Dutch puff (pancake), 226
in Easter rice, 215
in frittata, 223
hardboiled, 7, 31, 135, 171
in malfatti, 131
in zucchini casserole, 161
escarole: in greens and beans, 146
in wedding soup, 30

ferratelle. *See* pizzelles
fish: amberjack, 110
anchovies, canned, on pasta, 74, 79
in cioppino, 40
cod (dried, salted), salad, 175
flounder, baked, 109
grilled in foil, 108
haddock, baked, 109
oreganato, 109
perch, baked, 109
smelts, deep-fried, 18–19
snapper, in soup, 40
swordfish, stir-fried, with ginger and lemon grass, 110
tuna, canned, with pasta, 74
fresh, stir-fried, 110
frittata, 223
fritters, pumpkin flower, 153–54
fruit: for antipasto, 14
desserts, 208, 211–12, 212
slaw, 178
fudge, 220

bows, in salad, 171

bow ties, with shrimp, 80

capellini, with anchovies and garlic, 79

ditalini, with beans, 67, 71

in soup, 43

dough, 76–78

e fagiole. *See* pasta, fazool

fazool (pasta e fagiole), 67–68

with corn, 71–72

lasagna. *See* polenta lasagna

macaroni, and cheese, 152

white. *See* oily-oilies

manicotti, stuffed, 62

mostaccioli, with shrimp, 80

orzo, in soup, 42

penne, with shrimp, 80

ravioli malfatti. *See* malfatti

rotini, in salad, 171, 172, 173

salads, 171, 172, 173

shells, with beans, 71

in salad, 171

spaghetti, and meatballs, 63–64

spaghettini, with clam sauce, 73

with tuna, olives, and mushrooms, 74–75

vermicelli, with anchovies and garlic, 79

with tuna, olives, and mushrooms, 74–75

vodka, 80

see also noodles

peach and cake mix dessert, 213

peanut butter: in cookies, 194, 205

in pad thai, 139

squares, 205

peanuts, in cookies, 197

pear, Asian, in fruit slaw, 178

peas: canned, with onions, 136

soup of split, 44

pecans: in candy, 219

in cookies, 198

in salad, 168

pepper(s): fried, 157

green bell, and fish grilled in foil, 108

in soup, 34, 40, 42

stuffed, 102

and tomato pizza, 58–59

Italian green, and tomatoes, 99

jalapeno, in chili, 45

red bell, prepared roasted, 94

in Spanish rice, 130

in stuffed manicotti, 62

in salad, 170, 171, 173

see also chile; vinegar peppers

pepper jelly, and cream cheese appetizer, 10

pie, onion, 156

piecrust: graham cracker (pre-made), 207

saltine cracker, 156

pilaf, bulgur wheat and lentil, 122

pineapple: canned, in cookies, 190

in salad, 166, 167

and chicken, stir-fried, 90–91

and cream cheese salad, 166

orange and carrot salad, 167

pine nuts, 121, 172

pinzimonio, 16

pizza: breakfast, 224

crust, of frozen bread dough, 59

dough, 49–50, 58–59

fritte, 155

green pepper and tomato, 58–59

sauce, 49–50, 58–59

stuffed greens, 61

tomato and cheese, 49–51

pizzelles (brigidini; cialdi; ferratelle; waffles), 192, 193

polenta, 125–26

lasagna, 128

with sausage, 126

with vegetables, 127–28

pork: and beans, canned, in coogootz, 118, 119

roast, 106

potatoes: fried, 151

with mushrooms, 230

hash browns (frozen), on pizza, 224

in moussaka, 137

in polenta, 127

in soup, 43

in Swiss steak, 98

pressure cooker, 89

pudding mix, for zuppa inglese, 206

pumpkin: cookies, 189

flowers, fried (fritters), 153–54

quesadillas, 129

radishes, in pasta salad, 173

raisins: in braciole, 95

in cake, 209

in cookies, 190, 195

in Easter rice, 215

in salad, 168

in stuffing, 102, 113

ramen noodles: in chicken salad, 177

in slaw, 164

taco seasoning, for dip, 6
tahini, in spinach and beans, 121
Te-Tus cookies, 197
toffee, 219
tofu, in pad thai, 139
tomatoes: canned, in chicken cacciatore, 89
  in chili, 45
  with Italian peppers, 99
  in macaroni and cheese, 152
  in moussaka, 137
  with mushrooms, 176
  in pasta sauce, 63, 66, 67, 71, 80
  on pizza, 58
  with polenta, 126, 127
  in soup, 40, 42, 43
  in Spanish rice, 130
  for Swiss steak, 98
  fresh, and asparagus salad, 163
  on bruschetta, 8
  in coogootz, 119
  and Italian peppers, 99
  in manicotti, 62
  in pasta sauce, 71
  in salad, 170, 172, 173
  in soup, 34

in stuffed peppers, 102
  with zucchini and pork and beans (coogootz), 118
  sun-dried, in pasta salad, 172
tomato juice, canned, 34, 45
tomato paste: in chili, 45, 105
  in moussaka, 137
  in pasta sauce, 63, 66
tomato puree, 63, 66, 174
tomato sauce: canned, for coogootz, 118, 119
  for malfatti, 131
  for pasta, 67
  for pizza, 49
  with polenta, 126
  in Spanish rice, 130
  in chicken salad, 174
toppings, pizza, 49
tortillas, for quesadillas, 129
trifle, citrus, 212

vegetables: for antipasto, 14
  moussaka of, 137–38
  polenta with, 127–28
  soup, with sausage, 42
  see also specific vegetables
venison chili, 45
vinegar peppers, 174
  with pickled eggplant, 161
  in salad, 174, 175

vodka, 23, 24
  pasta, 80

waffles. *See* pizzelles
walnuts: and apple Bundt cake, 209
  in candy, 219
  and cherry dessert, 213
  in cookies, 195, 197
  and pasta, 79
  in salad, 168
wheat germ, in macaroni and cheese, 152
wine: with chicken, 89
  as marinade for beef, 92
  in pasta sauce, 66, 73
  in risotto, 109
  in sangria, 21
  in soup, 40, 43

yogurt, in spinach and beans, 121

zucchini: casserole, 160
  in coogootz, 120, 121
  in frittata, 223
  in macaroni and cheese, 152
  in moussaka, 137
  in polenta, 127
  in soup, 42
zuppa inglese, 206